The Life and Message of The Real Rain Man

The Journey of a Mega-Savant

Fran Peek
with Lisa L. Hanson

DUDE PUBLISHING
A Division of
National Professional Resources, Inc.
Port Chester, New York

Publisher's Cataloging-in-Publication
(Provided by Quality Books, Inc.)

Peek, Fran.
The life and message of the real rain man : the journey of a mega-savant / by Fran Peek ; with Lisa Lyn Hanson.
p. cm.
Includes bibliographical references.
ISBN-13: 978-1934032-17-6
ISBN-10: 1934032-17-4

1. Peek, Kim. 2. Peek, Fran. 3. Savants (Savant syndrome)—Biography. 4. Fathers and sons—Biography. 5. Savant syndrome. I. Hanson, Lisa Lyn. II. Title.

BF426.P43 2007 153.9'0922
QBI07-600128

Editor: Helene M. Hanson
Production Editor, Cover Design: Andrea Cerone,
National Professional Resources, Inc., Port Chester, NY

Dude Publishing
A Division of National Professional Resources, Inc.
25 South Regent Street
Port Chester, New York 10573
Toll free: (800) 453-7461
Phone: (914) 937-8879

Visit our web site: www.NPRinc.com

Printed in the United States of America

ISBN 978-1-934032-17-6

Acknowledgements

These special moments, trials and tribulations, social experiences, new involvements in brain and memory studies, times of humor and sadness, and much more, are dedicated to:

Kim's mother, Jeanne, and her husband, Gordon;
his brother Brian and Brian's wife, Lizz;
his sister, Alison, and her beloved dog, Jimmy;
his very special friend Mary Ruth (Gold Tooth);
and to the hundreds and thousands of our friends all over the world who have helped nurture the self-esteem, confidence, and talents of this very unique and loving person, my son, Kim.

Also, our appreciation to Barry Morrow, Dr. Daniel Christensen, Dr. Darold A. Treffert, Dr. April Greenan, Robert and Helene Hanson and the staff of National Professional Resources, Inc., and to Angela Hanson Garofalo who has become one of Kim's most special new friends; she is loved by both of us.

I am also particularly grateful to Lisa Hanson, my collaborator, whom I met only six short months ago. We immediately connected. When she and I initially discussed this book I knew that her insight, intelligence and sensitivity would serve me well…and how right I was!

—Fran Peek

Contents

Preface

Welcome to the journey of my son, Kim Peek, the prodigious intellectual memory savant who was the inspiration for the 1988 Academy Award-winning movie, *Rain Man*, which starred Dustin Hoffman and Tom Cruise, with the original script written by Barry Morrow.

Having grown from a reclusive child into an international celebrity, Kim now amazes throngs of people with his mega-savant abilities and inspires them with his commitment to the beautiful message of the Golden Rule. He punctuates this message with a call for universal acceptance of differences, recognizing that, "You don't have to be handicapped to be different."

Thanks to the talent and creativity of my collaborator, you will become a part of our lives, past and present. As you move forward on this journey of discovery, you will get to know my amazing son and, like all who meet him, be touched and moved by his uniqueness and naïve charm.

Enjoy the Journey!

Introduction

The classic movie, *Rain Man*, is not the story of my son, Kim Peek. Yet Kim is known around the world as "The Real Rain Man." He was screenwriter Barry Morrow's inspiration for creating the character, Raymond Babbitt (a.k.a. "Rain Man"), that earned Dustin Hoffman the 1988 Academy Award for Best Actor. But Raymond Babbitt is just that—a character, far less complex and far less astounding than my son Kim, who Morrow has called "perhaps the most unusual person who has ever lived."

Kim is a one-of-kind "mega-savant," whose abilities exceed those of other savants, such as the one portrayed in the movie *Rain Man*. Indeed, the character of Raymond Babbitt possesses only a fraction of Kim's extraordinary gifts and challenging disabilities.

Unlike most savants, Kim's extraordinary memory abilities extend to 15 different subjects areas, rather than just two or three. Known to many as "Kim-puter," his areas of savant memory include world and American history, sports, movies, geography, space programs, actors and actresses, the Bible, religion, literature, Shakespeare, classical music and opera. He knows all of the area codes and zip codes in the United States, together with the television stations serving those locales. He learns the maps in the front of phone books and can provide Yahoo-like travel directions within any major U.S. city or Canadian town, and between any pair of them. Kim likes to know the birthday of everyone he meets so that he can tell them—almost instantaneously—what day of the week they were born, what day of the week their birthday will fall on in the current year, and what year and day of the week it will be when they turn 65 (retirement age).

Kim has read over 12,000 books. Once he has read a book at lightning speed, he photographically retains the information and can recall and often recite it with 97 percent accuracy decades later. He can identify hundreds of classical music compositions, tell when and where each was composed and first performed, give the name of the composer and many biographical details, and even discuss the formal and tonal components of the music.

So, *Rain Man* does not tell Kim's story. Kim was never institutionalized. He was never reunited with a long-lost brother the way Raymond was reunited with his brother, Charlie (played by Tom Cruise) in the film. He has in fact been to the casinos in Las Vegas, but although he can count cards, he has no interest in gambling and won't play. If there is a Charlie to Kim's

Raymond, that would be me, his father. I am Kim's caretaker and companion, just as Charlie was to Raymond in the movie, but that's where the similarities end.

Kim and I have never driven across the country in a convertible Cadillac, but we have flown over 1,760,000 miles around the world and have driven nearly a million miles across the Western United States. Throughout our years of traveling, Kim has certainly posed his share of challenges, and, like Charlie in the movie, I have at times been impatient with Kim. But, just as Charlie found it impossible to not fall in love with his brother, people cannot help but fall in love with Kim. And no one loves Kim more than I do.

The movie *Rain Man,* released in 1988, won four Academy Awards (Best Picture; Best Actor, Dustin Hoffman; Best Director, Barry Levinson; Best Screen Play, Barry Morrow and Ron Bass) and changed our lives in unimaginable ways. It also helped change the way people in this country and around the world perceive individuals with disabilities. However, it has now been almost twenty years since *Rain Man* was released, and despite the fact that it stars a young Tom Cruise, many young people have never seen the movie. Their parents may not have seen it since it was in theaters close to two decades ago (although it is frequently shown on cable networks). Yet it is essential that the message of the movie not be lost, especially at a time when, more than ever, people with disabilities want and need to be included and accepted in every aspect of society.

Kim and I are committed to not letting the message of acceptance of others—*all* others, including those with disabilities—fade. Like Charlie, people best learn acceptance by meeting and interacting with individuals who are different from them. Just as Charlie learned to accept and even cherish his brother, people's preconceived notions are shattered when they interact with Kim and experience his gentle, caring soul and marvel at his incredible abilities.

Hundreds, sometimes thousands of people every month are introduced to Kim as he and I visit with various organizations, from school groups to professional conferences to retirement homes. We have met with over three and a half million people... but only in the past eighteen years. Prior to that time, before the movie *Rain Man*, Kim interacted with virtually no one outside of his immediate family. His mother and I wanted to protect him, and we probably would be doing so to this day were it not for Dustin Hoffman and *Rain Man* screenwriter Barry Morrow who insisted that we share our very special son with the world.

CHAPTER 1
A Very Unusual Childhood

Kim was born in Salt Lake City, Utah, on November 11, 1951 (a Sunday, he will quickly tell you). Although her pregnancy seemed reasonably normal, Kim's mother underwent a difficult labor preceding his birth. From the beginning we knew he was "different." His head was 30 percent larger than normal—so large that his neck muscles couldn't support it. He was sluggish and cried a lot. He didn't play, didn't respond to stimuli, didn't experience the normal stages of development. Each of his eyes moved independently of the other, and a soft, baseball-sized blister stretched across the back of his head on the right side, a growth doctors refused to touch for fear that it might be a part of his brain. Later, at age three, the blister quickly retracted, at the same time pulling a nodule into Kim's cerebellum and destroying part of it. Decades after the fact we learned that Kim had had an encephalocele (herniation of brain tissue through the skull) which spontaneously resolved, leaving him with considerable brain damage.

At nine months a doctor pronounced Kim mentally retarded and recommended that we place him in an institution and get on with our lives. We took him home.

Cuddling him in our arms or laying him on the sofa with his head propped up with pillows, we read to him, hour after hour, tracing the rows of words with his tiny finger as we went. And, in time, our so-called "retarded" infant son began displaying some remarkable abilities. For one, he took an early interest in books, apparently absorbing everything he heard, read and saw. However, because he was non-communicative, we would not discover the extent of his talents for several years.

At 18 months, he showed marked signs of being a creature of habit. For instance, he always insisted on turning the Little Golden Books upside-down once we had read them to him or he had looked through them himself, to separate them from unread material, a habit he maintains even today. (The way he explains it now, if the content is already committed to his memory, he no longer needs to refer to it.)

Physically, Kim developed slowly. He wasn't able to walk on his own until he was past four years old. Prior to that time, he would put his

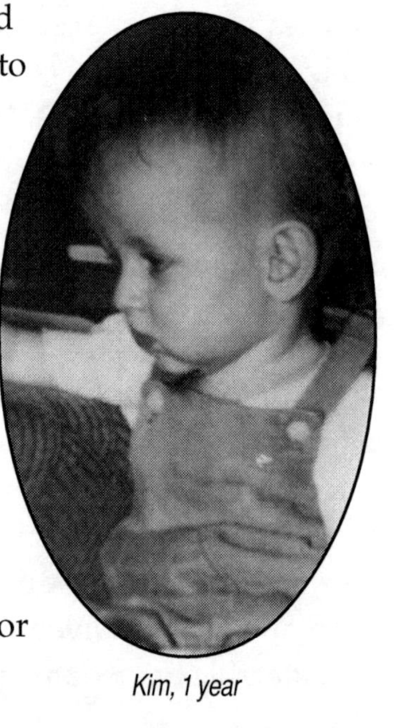

Kim, 1 year

forehead to the floor and crawl like a snowplow, unable to support his large and heavy head. He couldn't walk up and down the stairs on his own until he was 14 years old, making it necessary for me to carry him. When he did finally walk on his own, it was with a clumsy gait.

As a child he was rarely ill, which is likely attributable to his lack of social exposure during his childhood. He got measles and chicken pox along with his brother and sister and kids on our block, but he never fell seriously ill, which was fortunate because it is next to impossible to find out whether he hurts anywhere. In spite of Kim's developmental abnormalities, we always sensed that he possessed some special gift, some mental powers beyond our ability to explain.

The first signs of Kim's unique gifts surfaced when he was three years old. One day, when he was sitting on the floor browsing through the newspaper, he asked his mom and me, "What does 'con-fi-den-tial' mean?'" Without thinking, his mom jokingly told him to look up the word in the dictionary. He did. About 30 seconds after pulling himself up to the desk and selecting the dictionary, he found the word and asked us to read out the definition. We started watching him a little more closely after that!

At age five, Kim became obsessed with numbers and arithmetic, reading telephone directories and adding columns of telephone numbers. He enjoyed totaling the numbers on automobile license plates and identifying the model and type of every car we passed.

At age six, having already memorized the entire index of a set of encyclopedias, Kim was registered to begin first grade. He lasted a grand total of seven minutes in the classroom before he was turned away for being hyperactive and disruptive. The school principal advised his mother and me to "keep him at home where children like him belong." Shortly thereafter, doctors advised us to consider having him undergo a lobotomy. Of course, we declined.

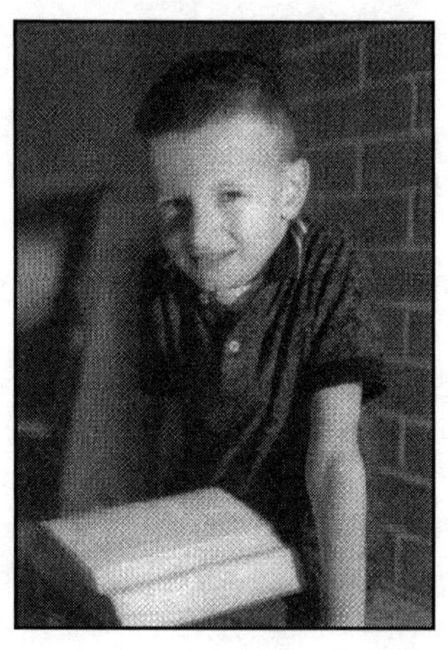

Kim, 1960

Kim was prescribed daily medications of Thorazine and Sandril to control his pacing and constant talking, yet he remained withdrawn and disruptive. At that time, attending school was clearly not an option for Kim, yet it was obvious to his mother and me that our son wanted and needed to learn. While his brother, sister and peers played and interacted with one another, Kim could usually be found cuddling magazines, newspapers and encyclopedias. His books were more dear to him than anything else in his life.

After our relentless appeals, the school district agreed to provide retired elementary school teachers as tutors for Kim (and four other children with retardation characteristics who had also been denied school attendance) for twice weekly, 45-minute sessions.

Once he began his lessons at age seven and a half, Kim progressed exceptionally quickly, often jumping ahead in his assignments. If he was assigned three pages of reading as homework on Tuesday and three pages on Thursday, he would likely finish reading the entire book in that time. I recall the tutor explaining to him that he did not have to read any more than three pages, to which he responded, "But if you start from the back and work to the front, it gets easier."

By the time he was 14 years old, Kim had completed the high school curriculum. In spite of his mastery of content, Kim did not officially graduate or receive his high school diploma at that time.

When he was 18, Kim got a job working on the payroll at the Columbus Community Center, a day workshop for adults with disabilities in Salt Lake City. Without the aid of calculators or computers, he prepared the payroll worksheet for the disabled employees at the center. The workshop contracts were piece-rate, with each of the eleven contracts in different amounts. Kim memorized each contract and multiplied the piece-per-item by the total number of items completed by each worker.

Kim doing payroll, 1969

In approximately six hours every other Tuesday and Wednesday, Kim calculated the payroll for some 160 workers so that they could be paid every other Friday. He faithfully and flawlessly performed his job for twelve years until the State of Utah mandated that payroll and account payable data for programs using state funds be processed through the state computer. After his payroll job was terminated, the workshop had to hire two full-time accountants to do the work he had done on a very part-time basis.

Kim's extraordinary abilities continued to astonish us as we noticed more and more instances of his genius intellect. In spite of his general reclusiveness, we also became increasingly aware of our son's tremendous sensitivity and generosity of spirit.

In May, 1970, when he was 19 years old, Kim was invited to participate in the 50-yard dash at the first Utah Special Olympics. Kim was very excited to participate and showed no signs of nervousness or insecurity, even though he had only learned to walk up and down stairs without assistance five short years before.

As he walked onto the track the day of the race, Kim was joined by two contestants in wheelchairs. Both young men had cerebral palsy and, like Kim, were anxious to win the gold metal. Aligned at the starting line, the pistol was raised into the air and the shot rang out to start the race.

Kim waited a few seconds as the two wheelchairs pulled quickly away from the starting line before beginning to run in his penguin-like, slightly sideward movement. He was soon several feet ahead of the other two struggling racers. One opponent was turning circles in an effort to propel his chair. The other, who had managed to sit backwards in his chair, was able to move a few feet with an occasional push of his feet.

With about six feet left to the 50-yard ribbon, Kim suddenly stopped. He turned around and saw the other two young men off to the side of the track, jammed together. I watched with pride as he walked back to them and pulled the wheelchairs apart. Slowly, he pushed the first chair through the ribbon. Then, he returned to the other racer, straightened out his chair, and pushed him across the finish line. Kim was a proud third place winner!

As he stood on the platform to receive his medal, Kim tilted his head back and forth as Coach Jack Curtis of the University of Utah football team placed the bronze medal over his head. Then, Coach Curtis took a second medal from the attendant and placed it over Kim's head.

"Kim," spoke the coach, "We hereby award you the most important recognition of the Special Olympics, the Sportsman Award, for your unselfishness in helping your two friends win the Gold and Silver medals in the 50-yard dash."

We were tremendously proud of our son's compassion and selflessness. Kim was accomplishing things, physically and emotionally, that we were told he would never accomplish. By the time he was a teenager, Kim had already outlived his predicted lifespan. He had read more books than most people read in a lifetime. However, even as a young adult, Kim remained unable to master the most simple activities of daily living such as showering, dressing, tooth-brushing, and making simple decisions.

Brian, Kim, and Alison, 1963

The early years of Kim's life were undoubtedly challenging for his brother and sister, both of whom were just a few years younger than he. They grew up in an environment that was often dictated by the special needs of their disabled sibling. His brother, Brian, who was more comfortable with Kim than was his sister, Alison, was sometimes willing to bring his friends to our home where they would meet and mingle with Kim. Brian shares now that he had no real idea of Kim's uniqueness until Kim became "Rain Man" and began speaking to schools.

Today, Brian and Alison enjoy reading articles about Kim's presentations and learning more about their brother from watching the documentaries that have been filmed worldwide. Brian was also amazed to discover, during a recent visit with Kim, that Kim actually remembered the names of some of his childhood friends. Kim does not talk about friends often, but does seem to truly enjoy his family: Brian, Alison, his mother, Jeanne, and her husband, Gordon.

In October of 1981, Kim's mother and I divorced. Whereas his mother had overseen most of Kim's care throughout his childhood, after the divorce I became Kim's primary caretaker. While Kim and I had always been quite close, he now depended on me for all of his many needs. Fortunately, Kim's mother is still very much a part of his life. They talk on the phone almost every day when we are home in Salt Lake City and I send her copies of materials related to our travels and presentations to keep her informed of our activities.

After our divorce, I made the decision to have Kim, then in his early 30's, further evaluated by medical professionals. Throughout his life we had known the nature, but not the cause, of his disabilities.

We also recognized that he had a host of exceptional abilities but no one, including myself, had any idea of the extent of his talents and how truly extraordinary Kim's gifts were.

Kim's social interactions, even with me, were quite impaired, and I yearned to understand more about how his brain worked and what might be going on in his remarkable mind. I also hoped that by gaining a better understanding of Kim we would be better able to help him, as well as potentially help others.

Kim and I were very fortunate during this time to have a very special friend, Mary Ruth—or, as Kim calls her, Mary Ruth with the Gold Tooth, because a shiny gold tooth glistened when she spoke. This lovely woman had been my executive secretary during the last 15 years of my service to the Utah State Office of Education. She became our total supporter and an important part of our lives, providing us with immeasurable encouragement and assistance. In concert with my widowed sister, Phyllis, she joined us on many travels and presentations. Kim once described the relationship of the four of us as three old apples and one young apple hanging on the same tree, and he would say, "If you want to pick one, you will have to take all four!"

I have frequently been asked why Mary Ruth and I did not marry. The reason is, my first priority in life was, and is, caring for and about Kim. I could not jeopardize that responsibility with any other relationship. Mary Ruth understood. She now suffers from dementia and lives in a care facility. Every day that we are in town I visit her, help her say her prayers and put her to bed. She continues to be tremendously special to both of us.

Mary Ruth (Gold Tooth) and Kim, 1987

CHAPTER 2
A One-of-a-Kind Brain; Possibly, a One-of-a-Kind Individual

In 1988, Dr. Daniel Christensen of the University of Utah Neuropsychiatric Institute conducted the first MRI scans of Kim's brain, and has continued to follow him ever since. These initial tests showed that Kim has a malformed cerebellum, which Christensen and others believe may account for his problems with coordination and mobility. The most striking finding was the absence of a corpus callosum, the sizable stalk of nerve tissue that normally connects the left and right halves of the brain. It has been conjectured that Kim may owe some of his talents to this particular abnormality.

Dr. Christensen explains that the corpus callosum is a bundle of fibers that allows the left brain to "talk" to the right brain. Completely lacking these fibers, Kim's left brain is unable to communicate with his right brain. In an interview for the Swedish documentary *Verklighetens Rainman* (2006), Christensen marveled at this finding: "This is one of the very interesting aspects of Kim's situation. You would expect almost to find something extra in his brain, something that gave him a talent or a memory that you or I don't have, but you don't see it. You see a brain that looks... damaged."

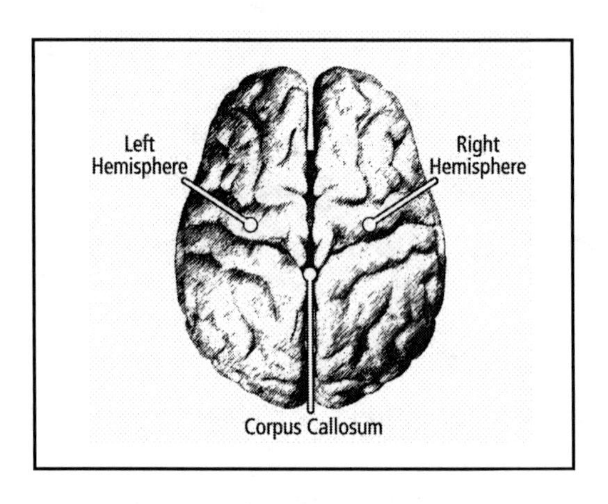

Imaging studies have also revealed a complex, rare optical system that enables Kim to read two pages in paperback-type books simultaneously in about eight to ten seconds, with almost total recall. He can also read single pages by focusing both eyes on the material. Kim reads a page that takes an average person about three minutes to read in less than 30 seconds. He spends more time on the pages of almanacs, maps, or other materials that require concentration, probably focusing on the material with both eyes at the same time. While reading, he often makes monotone droning noises. These noises appear to be part of his concentration process and drown out any outside distractions.

He has semblances of dyslexia as well, and is able to read things that are upside-down, sideways, or mirror-imaged. His brain has somehow "recircuited itself" to accomplish awesome capabilities. We had heard the term "savant" and "idiot savant" over the years, but Kim had not received an official diagnosis beyond mental retardation up to this time.

Savant Syndrome is a fascinating and still puzzling condition which Dr. Darold Treffert, an expert on Savant Syndrome, defines as, "a condition in which persons with a major mental illness or major intellectual handicap have spectacular islands of ability and brilliance that stand in stark, startling contrast to those handicaps" (Treffert, D., 2006, pp. 2-3).

Dr. Treffert has worked with savants for over 40 years and is the author of a comprehensive book on Savant Syndrome entitled, *Extraordinary People: Understanding Savant Syndrome.* In this book, as well as on his website, www.savantsyndrome.com, Treffert discusses in detail the past theories and current understanding of Savant Syndrome.

Dr. Darold Treffert

Individuals who today are said to have Savant Syndrome were previously considered "idiot savants." At the time this term was coined in the late 1800's by Dr. J. Langdon Down of London, the word "idiot" did not have a derogatory or negative connotation; rather, it was simply an accepted medical and psychological term referring to a specific level of intellectual functioning. The word "savant" was derived from a French word meaning "to know," or, "man of learning." The term "idiot savant" was a juxtaposition of these two words, describing persons with severe mental handicaps who displayed advanced levels of learning (Treffert, D., 2006, p. 2). Fortunately, this term is no longer used.

Dr. Treffert categorizes persons with Savant Syndrome as being either "talented savants" or "prodigious savants." Whereas talented savants exhibit skills that are remarkable simply in contrast to their handicap, prodigious savants, who are much rarer, possess abilities and skills that would be remarkable even if viewed in normal persons (Treffert, D., 2006, p. 3).

Kim clearly falls into the latter category of prodigious savant. There have been less than 100 prodigious savants reported in all of world literature. In most cases, the prodigious savant's extraordinary brilliance occurs within a very narrow range. Kim is unique even among this spectacular population in that his phenomenal memory extends to over fifteen subject areas from world history, to music, sports, religious texts, Shakespeare and more.

Savant Syndrome often presents in individuals who are autistic; however not all savants are autistic, and not all individuals with autism are savants. Returning to reflections from the movie *Rain Man*, this is another way in which the character of Raymond Babbitt differs from Kim. In the film, Raymond was an autistic savant. While some of Kim's behavioral characteristics are similar to autistic behaviors, he does not fit the profile of an individual with autism, although for a time prior to his socialization some conjectured that he was in fact autistic. It was not until after *Rain Man* was released that Kim was diagnosed as a prodigious memory savant with autistic characteristics but not Autism Spectrum Disorder.

In *Extraordinary People*, Dr. Treffert makes the distinction between autism as a condition (now referred to as Autism Spectrum Disorder), which is present at birth and characterized by profound withdrawal, an obsessive desire for sameness, absence of affectionate relationships with others, mutism or language that does not seem to serve any useful interpersonal purpose, and autism as a symptom, which refers to the presence of autistic behaviors in a person with a variety of disorders, including brain damage and subsequent developmental disability (Treffert, D., 2006, p. 17).

About 50 percent of savants have brain damage of some sort, often present at birth, and they can have, superimposed on that, autistic symptoms, without having Autism Spectrum Disorder. That is the case with Kim. Some autistic behaviors and mannerisms (symptoms) are superimposed on, or concurrent with, his basic underlying organic brain dysfunction.

In addition to lacking a corpus callosum, studies of Kim's brain have revealed abnormalities in the left hemisphere. It has been explained that the right hemisphere of the brain can more easily derive meaning from concrete objects or events that are directly perceived whereas the left hemisphere is primarily understood to be symbolic-conceptual, dealing with functions that use logical, symbolic, abstract strategies and methods (Treffert, D. 2006, p. 191). The theory of left-brain/right-brain specialization would therefore appear to account, at least in part, for Kim's difficulty with abstract thinking.

The nature of the savant-type memory is automatic, mechanical, concrete and habit-like. Dr. Treffert notes that, "when one examines the correlation here between the types of functions that tend to be associated with one hemisphere or the other, and the types of symptoms and behavior seen in the savant… one sees a predominance of right brain function in this condition" (2006, p. 192).

Some in the scientific community attribute savant skills to left hemisphere abnormalities or damage, hypothesizing that when the left hemisphere cannot function properly, the right hemisphere compensates by developing new skills, perhaps by recircuiting brain tissue normally earmarked for other purposes. Another possibility is that injury to the left hemisphere merely unveils skills that had been latent in the right hemisphere all along.

Kim's deficiencies in left hemisphere-related skills involving symbolic and conceptual thinking were demonstrated in a documentary on Kim entitled *The Real Rain Man* (2006). This program includes footage of Kim participating in a test used to assess an individual's ability to relate information and develop conceptual associations. For this test, a list of 15 words was read to Kim: sour, candy, sugar, bitter, good, taste, tooth, nice, honey, soda, chocolate, heart, cake, tart, pie. All of these words are related to the concept of sweet, yet the word "sweet" was not actually on the list. According to Professor V.S. Ramachandran of U.C. San Diego, 98 percent of people to whom this test is administered would say that sweet was on the list of words because they would focus on the concept and conceptually encode the information. Kim, on the other hand, correctly remembered that the word "sweet" was in fact not on the original list, which suggests that, unlike most other subjects, he did not relate the words to the concept of sweet.

Another indication of left brain deficiency is the fact that Kim does not understand metaphors. Consistent with right brain dominance, Kim thinks very literally. For example, if you tell Kim to "get a grip" on himself, he will understand this to mean he should hold onto himself and will respond by physically grabbing himself. When a researcher asked Kim what it means to "follow in your father's footsteps," he responded, "Hold Dad's arm so I won't get lost in the airport." He does not seem to comprehend the symbolic, metaphorical implications of common expressions such as these.

This literal way of thinking impaired Kim's performance on his first IQ test in 1988. Based on his responses, Kim's IQ was calculated to be 74, the range within which most mentally retarded individuals score. When I discussed the specifics of the testing with one of the psychologists, he expressed the opinion that this score was not indicative of Kim's true abilities. Rather, it better represented his inability to cope with abstract thinking. His interpretations of and answers to questions related to metaphors and to math problems were, to say the least, atypical. His responses simply did not conform to the expectations of the testing protocols. Kim apparently had taken every word and expression from the test as being literal in every way. He is so totally honest that practical, absolute answers and applications govern every facet of his reasoning. His mind, similar to a computer's hardware, can only perceive reality and hard fact.

Consistent with his literal-mindedness, Kim doesn't like to talk about mathematics, chemistry or other very technical subjects. Although he knows all of the nation's area codes and what telephone companies serve each region, he won't reveal people's specific phone numbers and addresses.

Because the character in the movie *Rain Man* could do lighting calculations, people often assume that Kim has this ability as well and will ask him to perform complex mathematical equations, expecting a rapid response. They are surprised to find that, in fact, Kim does not do math. When he is asked to solve math problems he simply and unashamedly declines. My own suspicion is that this is a matter of choice rather than an inability to perform calculations. After all, Kim was a wizard at calculating payroll for his job for over 15 years, never using a calculator.

The only time I recall Kim answering a calculation question was when Dustin Hoffman asked,

"Kim, if I asked you what 320 times 160 is, could you tell me?"

"You double the top number, halve the bottom number, double the top, halve the bottom, double the top, halve the bottom, double the top, halve the bottom, double the top, halve the bottom, and then multiply the top number, 5120, by the bottom number, 10, and you have 51,200. But I don't do math problems."

Although he will not do math problems, one of Kim's favorite talents is calculating dates. This is a common skill among savants, many of whom do not have savant abilities in math. Dr. Treffert believes that Kim and other savants do not use math to perform calendar calculations.

May
Su Mo Tu We Th Fr Sa
1 2 3
4 5 6 7 8 9 10
11 12 13 14 15 16 17
18 19 20 21 22 23 24
25 26 27 28 29 30 31

1981

1968

January
Su Mo Tu We Th Fr Sa
1 2 3
4 5 6 7 8 9 10
11 12 13 14 15 16 17
18 19 20 21 22 23 24
25 26 27 28 29 30 31

1913

October
Su Mo Tu We Th Fr Sa
1 2
3 4 5 6 7 8 9
10 11 12 13 14 15 16
17 18 19 20 21 22 23
24 25 26 27 28 29 30
31

1946

2032

November
Su Mo Tu We Th Fr Sa
1
2 3 4 5 6 7 8
9 10 11 12 13 14 15
16 17 18 19 20 21 22
23 24 25 26 27 28 29
30

2009

1997

> Calendar calculating, and lightning calculating (the ability to multiply or divide huge numbers very rapidly, or derive prime numbers), are two different savant skills. It is impressive (and puzzling) to me why calendar calculating, an obscure skill in most of us, is almost universally present in savants. Most savants who calendar calculate do so unconsciously, or pre-consciously, with no idea how they do it. While some lightning calculating savants 'do math,' others, like Kim, do not 'do math.' The formula or algorithm for calendar calculating somehow spontaneously appears in savants, or is unconsciously inculcated by studying the set patterns in calendars. I don't know how Kim obtained his capacity to calendar calculate, but that's not an uncommon circumstance with calendar calculators. I don't know how they do it, either. But calendar calculating and lightning calculating are two different skills. While both may appear in some savants, that is not usually the case (Treffert, D., Personal Email, April 2, 2007).

Some three years after Kim's initial IQ testing was performed, several psychologists decided to reevaluate his mental capabilities. Considering the uniqueness of Kim's learning abilities, his inventory of information and his inability to weigh most abstract information, his "knowledge quotient" (substituted for the normal IQ identification) was calculated to be in the realm of 184, plus or minus 5 points, which would put him in the highest genius range.

Kim as a young man

Kim and I live in Salt Lake City, Utah, as does Kim's mother, Jeanne. Like many in our area, Kim's mother and her family are devout Mormons. My parents were also converts to the Church of Jesus Christ of Latter-day Saints. People have asked me whether Kim is religious or has an understanding of God. The short answer would have to be no. Because of his reasoning limitations, I think that Kim's religion is what he has read and heard, not what he contemplates and theorizes. Being fact-oriented, he doesn't express feelings or opinions about faith-based religion. As a matter of fact, Kim does not express opinions about most things. When people ask him who/what his "favorite" person or thing is, he usually responds, "I like them all."

Psychologists have asked me if Kim can tell fact from fiction, because in addition to non-fiction, he does read some classic novels. Although he is very fact-oriented, he understands the concept of a story and knows that stories are made up and not real. When he reads Shakespeare or Dickens, for example, he is able to recognize that the content is different from the information in history books, probably because he knows everything about Shakespeare and Dickens and all of the other playwrights and authors he reads, including the fact that they are famous for their creative works and are not historians. However, for the most part, Kim is not interested in fiction unless it has historical or literary merit.

Doctors and scientists have multiple theories but few definite answers to the question of exactly how savants are able to do what they do. In addition to the theory of right brain/left brain specialization, it is believed that savants might have "an inability to forget rather than a special capacity to remember" (Treffert, D., 2006, p. 203). This theory stems from the fact that savants such as Kim demonstrate "impressive long-term memory for what is usually short term material for the rest of us, material such as phone numbers or assorted trivia. There is, then a conspicuous inability to forget and to erase. The insignificant facts remain and actually obscure and block pathways to more long-term, more typically associative memory" (Treffert, D., 2006, p. 203). Thus, this kind of memory can be understood as a failure of one aspect of memory and an excess of another.

In a documentary about Kim for Swedish television entitled *Verklighetens Rainman* (2006), Dr. Christensen speculates, "The issue [with Kim] isn't that he can store so much more; the issue is he has access to it. If we only knew how to tap it, I would guess that you remember many, many things that you don't have access to like that, but you can't just go back in and grab it. And my guess is, with Kim, it's simply… he has no barriers there. He just has ready access to anything that's gone in."

For example, Kim likes to listen to music. Once he hears a musical selection from a record, tape, or live presentation, he is able to hum it, describe it, and provide considerable information about the composer and other facts about the music… even if it's been 30 or 40 years since he has heard it!

He also enjoys reading the record jackets and labels, or the tape/CD boxes. He recalls where a selection appears on the record or tape, the publisher, and, usually, the color of the label. Kim seems unable to forget things he has heard or read since he was two or three years old. And not only is the information retained in his brain, but it seems to be filed away for immediate recall.

Dr. Treffert refers to a savant's memory as "a procedural or automatic memory that's exceedingly deep. Information is received and then it automatically and unconsciously goes to his 'hard disk' and is stored there" (Nilsson, A., 2006).

Treffert, who continues to study Savant Syndrome and still closely follows Kim, writes:

> Savant memory, I suspect, is just that—a highly developed, compensatory noncognitive, alternate pathway developed to compensate for injury to or absence of the more usual and more frequently used cognitive memory seen in the

> rest of us. Savant memory is almost devoid of emotion, is automatic and nonvolitional, is certainly not reflective or highly associative and could well be that "habit" system.... a cortico-striatal "habit" system may well be the naturally available alternative in the savant. (Treffert, D., 2006, p. 223)

In layman's terms, the "habit system" is more a system of reflexes than conscious memory. Kim does not study material or attempt to memorize facts with the intent to be able to recall information. He simply reads something once and then he remembers it exactly, without putting in any effort. It's as if his brain is a camera and once he has snapped the photograph he can simply refer back to it. He doesn't struggle to remember the information, it's just readily available to him. For Kim, reading *is* memorizing. When he is asked what day of the week it will be on October 12, 2097 (a Saturday, he tells me) he doesn't strain and "think" about the answer or try to work it out; he is just able to access that information.

Habit memory has also been described as memory without consciousness. It would be like you or me driving a car. At first, we have to learn the process: we learn how to shift gears, accelerate, brake, signal, steer, and any number of other required functions. In the early stages of learning to drive we have to concentrate carefully and consciously think about what we're doing and how to get ourselves safely to our destination. With some practice, however, this process becomes part of our habit memory. We don't have to "think" about what we're doing any more... we just know how to do it and can do it automatically. Soon, we can drive while changing the CD in the car stereo, talking on the cell phone, smoking a cigarette—none of which are recommended, by the way! Once we've "got it," whatever "it" might be, we are able to carry out the activity more automatically, with less conscious thought and attention. This demonstrates migration from one brain area to another, and from semantic memory (memory for concepts, facts, rules, etc.) to "habit memory" or "memory without reckoning." (Treffert, D., 2007).

When you stop to think about the number of things we do in a day, or even in an hour, and how automatic so much of our behavior is, it's really quite amazing. The "ordinary" mind is itself quite extraordinary. Just think of what our brains have to process merely to get ready to go to work every day: We are woken up by the alarm clock and without thinking we immediately know to reach over and hit the snooze button. We don't stop to think about what to do to make the beeping noise stop—we just do it. We know that to make the hot water come out of the faucet we need to turn the knob on the shower and wait a couple of minutes for the temperature to adjust. As we shower, we're probably thinking about that crazy dream we had last night, what we'll eat for breakfast, how much time we have to get to work, what we will wear today. We're not thinking about lathering the soap or rinsing the shampoo out of our hair.

After our shower we have to decide what clothes to wear. We do not have to think about what we will need; we know that we will need to choose underwear, socks, a shirt, pants, shoes, and maybe a jacket and tie. We do not make any effort to remember what articles of clothing are required. Likewise, we don't need to refer to directions when we get to the bus stop. We know to take out the fare, step onto the bus, deposit the fare into the fare box, and take a seat. If we want to say good morning to the bus driver we do not need to make an effort to find the right words or remember how to manipulate our tongues to produce the right sounds. These are all functions of our habit memory.

Kim's mind, like the minds of many savants, is not encumbered with all of this mundane yet very important information. He therefore has more immediate access to the information he has read in books, and even the sounds he has heard throughout his lifetime. Yet he lacks the "knowledge" to carry out basic activities required for independent living.

For neuro-typical individuals like you and me, the vast stores of habit memory and automatic processes that we call upon countless times throughout the day, allowing us to function as independent adults, are readily available… but at a price. We are able to access extensive practical habit memory at the expense of other "memory" or knowledge. We seem to "forget" obscure facts and details of the sort that Kim and other prodigious memory savants remember, because it is buried beneath massive amounts of other, more practical data.

Drs. Allan Snyder and D. John Mitchell of the Centre for the Mind in Australia believe that "the mechanisms for certain savant skills reside equally in all of us but cannot normally be accessed" (qtd. in Treffert, D. & Wallace, G., 2002). Essentially, they propose that savant skills represent brain processes that occur (or could occur) in each of us regularly, but they are swamped and buried by more sophisticated conceptual cognition and thus, savant-like capabilities remain largely at an unconscious level. Autistic savants, they conclude, "have privileged access to lower levels of information not normally available through introspection... we all have the same raw information but just cannot directly access it, at least on call" (qtd. in Treffert, D., 2007).

Dr. Treffert likewise believes that in each of us some of the same circuitry and pathways intrinsic to savant functioning still exist, but are not accessed. "It appears in some instances in each of us it is possible to tap different areas of Central Nervous System functioning than are typically or customarily used with a freeing up of, and possibility of tapping into, dormant abilities and habit memory capabilities." (Treffert, D. & Wallace, G., 2002) The question, then, is how to tap into this potential.

"Kim's story tells us that the human brain is far more flexible than we had thought," Dr. Treffert, told *The Observer* (December 11, 2005). "Like many other savants, he has suffered disability in one area of his brain, but has compensated by acquiring remarkable new abilities in other areas. This shows we all have considerable hidden intellectual potential. By studying Kim and other savants, we can learn how to tap those powers."

Although Dr. Treffert is an authority on savants and has met with many from around the world, he is nonetheless particularly in awe of Kim.

> All savants have a remarkable memory, but Kim's memory is like no other person's memory… and I've looked in the literature in the past 145 years and there is no other case like his in history, either… It's the rapidity with which he stores information, the fidelity with which he stores it, and the magnitude with which he stores it is simply unprecedented (Hofer, P. & Rockenhaus, F., 2006).

In the case of the prodigious savant, Treffert believes that there is "a marvelous coalescence of idiosyncratic brain circuitry, perhaps involving right hemisphere and habit memory compensatory processes, coupled with magnificent innate 'software,' obsessive traits of concentration and repetition, and tremendous encouragement and reinforcement from family, caretakers and teachers" (www.savantsyndrome.com).

It is of the utmost importance to note Dr. Treffert's assertion that savant abilities are enhanced by encouragement and reinforcement from family, caretakers and teachers. Thankfully, Kim's mother and I did not accept the early diagnoses of mental retardation rendering Kim incapable of learning. Although we could not imagine the extent of his abilities in those early years, we instinctively knew that he must at least be given the opportunity to learn. Imagine if we had decided to abide by the recommendation of Kim's early physicians who said that we should send him off to an institution to live out his life with nothing more than attention to his basic physical needs! What would have filled up that vast space in his brain that currently stores, with intricate detail, the contents of upwards of 12,000 books and countless newspapers, magazines, phone directories, almanacs, and musical compositions?

There are still many unanswered questions about how Kim does what he does and how his brain works. In fact, there are still a lot of answers about how the human brain works in all of us, and individuals and organizations in the medical and scientific communities are eager to find clues that will reveal more about this complex and remarkable organ.

One of the most exciting projects we've participated in has been a study of Kim's brain by researchers at the Center for Bioinformatics Space Life Sciences at the Salinas Valley Memorial Hospital in Salinas, California, in a joint project with NASA's Ames Research Center (NASA's Center of Excellence for Information Technology).

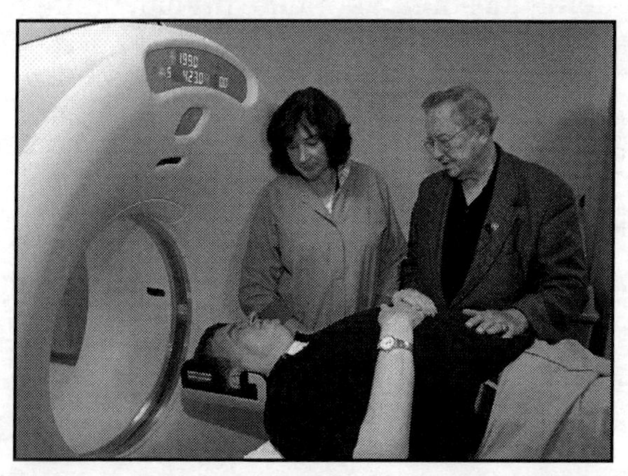

Photo by: Richard Green / Salinas Valley Memorial Healthcare System, 2004

This project, which began in 2004, involved Kim undergoing a number of painless and harmless scanning techniques, including computerized tomography and functional magnetic resonance imaging, in order to create a three-dimensional anatomical model of his brain. Richard Boyle, director of the NASA BioVIS Technology Center, describes the project as part of a larger effort to overlay and fuse image data from as wide a range of brains as possible, making Kim's unusual brain of particular value.

The data, both static and functional, should enable investigators to locate and identify changes in the brain that accompany thought and behavior. NASA hopes that this detailed model will enable physicians to improve their ability to interpret output from far less capable ultrasound imaging systems, which are the only kind that currently can be carried into space and used to monitor astronauts.

In addition to specific implications regarding astronauts and the effect of space travel on the brain, researchers also hope the tests will help answer some more general questions about the human brain, from its origin to how it works. One interest the researchers have is to look at a series of MRI images taken back in 1988 by Dr. Christensen in Utah and compare them to his brain today to see what has changed. Boyle has noted that Kim seems to be getting smarter in his specialty areas as he ages (to me there is no doubt of this) and suspects his brain images will reflect this change.

CHAPTER 3
The Public Journey Begins

While Kim's mind is unfathomably complex and his "island of genius" unprecedentedly vast, these aspects of his being do indeed stand in stark contrast to his significant and challenging disabilities and make it necessary for me to care for him much like one would a child.

After my divorce from Kim's mother, I took on the role of single parent and sole caregiver. Although he was an adult, Kim was (and still is) unable to bathe, shave and dress himself. Like a child, he could not be left alone. Because we had sought to shelter and protect him as a child, he was unaccustomed to interacting with anyone other than his immediate family and was uncomfortable with strangers; therefore, I did not feel I could leave Kim in anyone else's care, other than his Aunt Phyllis for short periods of time. Of course, this presented great logistical challenges. I could not stay at home with Kim around the clock. I needed to work and could not possibly live a totally secluded life. The only choice I had was to start taking Kim with me to public places for the first time in his life.

One of the first public places that Kim visited and responded well to was the public library. In fact, today the main Salt Lake City Public Library is literally a second home to Kim. While he was initially uncomfortable with people he encountered, he was in his glory surrounded by stacks and stacks of books, periodicals and directories. I found that I could take Kim to the library and actually relax a bit! I didn't need to watch him like a hawk or keep him from wandering. As soon as he sat down with reading material he was completely engrossed for hours upon hours.

Kim & Fran: Salt Lake City Library, 2006

It was from our trips to the library that I first became aware of an interesting and puzzling phenomenon. The man who could remember the most intricate and obscure facts about all kinds of subjects was not able to remember the simple matter of where our car was parked!

Kim and I started spending so much time at the library that he was soon familiar to the library staff. After several months of almost daily visits, I asked Kim what he thought about staying there with his books for a short time while I left to do some errands. The library staff always welcomed Kim and I knew that they would keep an extra-special eye on him. As I expected, Kim was so engrossed once amidst the stacks of books and reference materials, he didn't even miss me when I left him!

Today, the library remains one of Kim's favorite places. When we are not traveling Kim visits the library almost every weekday from 4 to 7:15 p.m. He is always engaged in some project, often privately recording information in a journal he keeps.

Kim favors routines, and his activities at the library are relatively consistent. He meanders into the reference sections behind the library staff desks, seeking out a specific book. Every now and then, his mouth broadens into an enthusiastic grin as he happens upon a book he hasn't yet explored.

His pacing quickens. He's in his comfort zone, very much at home in this, one of his favorite haunts, amid the throng of regular patrons and library staff (all of whom know him well, watch over him, and are accustomed to his unbroken chatter). Yet at the same time he's also very much alone as he roams among the flow of strangers ranging from a well-dressed businesswoman to a ragged transient.

He's encased in his own world, a faraway preoccupation with books. Thinking aloud, mumbling to himself in soft undertones, he shuffles mechanically on down the aisle in his customary penguin-like gait, his dronings echoing faintly for yards around. "Or less... or less," he repeats in a rhythmic delivery. Pausing in an awkward stance and picking up a familiar reference book, he chuckles, ticks off a series of numbers, then mutters to no one in particular, "You can check it out."

Finding an empty seat, he settles back with several massive reference catalogs he has collected in his wanderings. Gently spreading the pages of one of the volumes, he removes his black rimmed, thick-lens glasses and places them on the table. Then he positions the elongated tip of his nose about six inches from the page, squints his eyes, and begins reading, exhaling audibly with each breath, a low, guttural engine-revving noise. This sort of droning focuses his concentration and frees him from outside distractions.

Half an hour later, he carefully replaces the catalogs and retreats to a narrow row of phone directories. Removing one of the thick volumes and opening his red three-ring notebook marked with his name in large block letters, he sits down and finds the spot where he left off the last time (residents of Boise, Idaho—next week it might be an obscure town in Minnesota). The index finger of his right hand navigates precisely along a line of data, and he leans forward and to the right to let his left hand do the work. Deftly clutching a pencil, he begins scratching out row after row of names, each followed by an address, city, state, zip code, and phone number—minutia not merely committed to the pages of a dollar notebook, but also to his own computer-like memory.

The minutes stretch into an hour, and finally his jottings cease. He hoists the directory back into its place and scurries off once more, this time bee-lining to a shelf filled with reference books to check out a thick work titled *Chronicle of the 20th Century.*

Kim in Salt Lake City Library, 2006

Settling into a nearby chair, he laces his fingers in front of his face and gazes at and through them, a ritual he repeats several times an hour. He opens the book and begins studying the history of the early 1900's. He pours over the pages swiftly, while occasionally mumbling a date or name. With each breath, he emits a slightly new sound—a soft whistle, a whine, a high throaty groan, or a low giggle.

In his seemingly erratic searchings, he comes across an article on Russia's "Bloody Sunday" of 1905 and peruses it in depth. Then, between soft, higher-pitched groans, he slowly begins citing a list of dates: "February 24th, March 6th, April 7th…"

He flips over another fact-packed page about every thirty seconds. "June 24th (groan)… July 15th…"

Every now and then, he quizzes himself on a date or place, the answers spilling from his lips as if he's taking an open-book quiz and the answer is right in front of him (though by then he's turned several pages beyond that particular bit of information).

He turns back to his work and is about to proceed to the next page when something catches his eye: "August 17th." And finally, jiggling his knees and stamping his feet in delight he announces, "September 10th!" He skips forward to the year 1906, pleased at his accomplishment.

The routine continues as Kim whizzes through page after page, his head cocked to the side like a robin listening for a worm: "January 29th… April 19th… San Francisco earthquake… June 10th, 1919… July 17th. School children … August 22nd… Mona Lisa stolen…"

Every now and then, he issues a faint moan that slowly rises into a deep chuckle, followed by a minute of silence. His head swivels back and forth along the pages, his eyes tracking one historical fact after another. His bottom lip protrudes in a permanent pout and he shakes his right hand every now and again as if emptying his body of its excess buildup of energy.

Finally, another chuckle rumbles from deep in his throat, once again setting in motion a series of mumblings and browsing. Minutes later, with the wide crease of a smile spreading over his face, he cries out in simple triumph, "April threeeee!"

Here is clearly a man who loves learning for its own sake. Then, just like that, the search changes course. He's unearthed—perhaps out of something he just read or something he read months ago—a certain month and day: November 8th. But since it appears that the exact year eludes him, he begins flipping pages and scanning through each year's summary of events, whispering some dates under his breath, until he comes across the year, 1923, when Hitler was arrested after a failed coup attempt.

Roughly three hours after he first climbed from the car and ambled through the building's double doors, it's time to go home. Finding him deep in his studies at one of these customary third or fourth-floor tables, I ask him what exactly it is he's looking for. "I start with a certain day and advance until there's nothing left over," he explains. "Just advancing…"

Back in his pre-*Rain Man* days, Kim spent most of his time either at home reading, at the library working on his private projects, or occasionally accompanying me to meetings, where he was generally well behaved. Mostly he would stay by my side and sway from side to side, occasionally talking to me (whether or not I was already engaged in conversation), often talking to himself or making his familiar droning sounds. He never made eye contact with other people and did not respond when spoken to by anyone he didn't know.

On occasion I would be called upon to speak or appear at meetings and conferences out of state. Once in a while I was able to leave Kim for short periods in the care of my sister, Phyllis, or our dear friend Mary Ruth, but most of the time I declined out of town invitations, feeling that long distance travel would be too much for Kim. However, after he had become accustomed to attending local functions with me, I determined that he would probably be able to accompany me on an out of town trip.

When I first started traveling with Kim I was concerned for his safety. One of Kim's autistic characteristics is that he tends to wander, seemingly in an attempt to expel some of the extra energy he possesses. At home, I am happy to let Kim pace around the house. It's good exercise for him, particularly because he isn't able to keep his balance on a treadmill or climbing hills or running. Our home has three stories with 15 steps between each floor. Kim goes up and down the 30 steps at least 15-20 times daily.

However when we are in public places, especially large, crowded places such as an airport, Kim's wandering tendencies are potentially dangerous and were initially a source of significant anxiety for me. At the beginning of our airport travels, I attached a 12-foot cord to my belt and to his belt so he wouldn't wander off to talk to someone or read the signs and look at the posters. Parents of children with special needs—and any parents of young children—understand the fear of a child getting lost and know that there is nothing they wouldn't do to protect their child. I'm sure some people in the airport thought we were crazy—two adult men tethered together at the waist—but this system was effective and, after a few months, I was able to do away with the cord and trust Kim not to leave my side. Today, because we travel quite a lot, Kim and I have an agreement: Kim holds my left arm when outside our home.

CHAPTER 4
The Genesis of *Rain Man*

In 1984, Kim accompanied me on a trip to the Arlington, Texas headquarters of the National Association of Retarded Citizens (Arc). At the time I was serving as volunteer chairman of the organization's communications committee and we were meeting to discuss ways of increasing nationwide awareness of The Arc and its local chapters through public service announcements and other marketing vehicles.

Barry Morrow, whom I would later come to know as one of the most talented, personable and caring individuals I have ever met, had been invited by the Arc's director of communications to assist our committee. Morrow, a prominent screenwriter who a few years earlier had been honored with two of television's prestigious Emmy awards for writing the TV movie, *Bill,* and its sequel, *Bill II* (starring Mickey Rooney as a retarded college coffee shop manager who touched the hearts of a circle of university students), had accepted the invitation.

Barry came into the meeting at about 9:00 a.m. Kim, normally a recluse in such settings, came up behind Barry and tapped him on the shoulder. Barry turned around to find Kim close in front of him. Looking him square in the eyes, Kim said, "Barry Morrow, think about yourself!" Stunned, Barry just stood there for a moment. Then he turned to me and said, "Wow! That's some greeting! May I take him out in the hallway for a few minutes?"

Barry Morrow and Kim, 1991

Several hours later they returned. "Where did you get this guy?" Barry wanted to know. "We went over to the computer center and corrected some of the ZIP codes on the membership lists. Then we went into the library and Kim knew just about every author and every book on the shelves."

But that wasn't all that had impressed Barry. "Next," he continued, "we talked about baseball. You know, I'm a member of a sports club in Los Angeles, and I figure I have a pretty good knowledge of the game. Well, now I know someone who knows a lot more about it than I ever will!"

"Then, after discussing a little football, basketball, boxing and even horse racing, Kim went on to tell me what roads I should take on my way back to Claremont, California, where I live. He told me what cities I'd pass through, their area codes and ZIP codes—he even told me my phone number and some facts about Claremont!"

By now Barry's enthusiasm was overflowing. "I also told him my date of birth and he gave me the day of the week I was born, the day of the week my birthday will fall on this year, and the day of the week and year I will turn 65 so I can retire. We also discussed events of the Revolutionary War, the Civil War, World Wars I and II, Korea, and Vietnam. No way could one person know that much. No way!"

Barry then looked me in the eye and his voice took on a serious tone. I had no way of knowing at the time, but this was about to be a turning point in our lives. "You know, Fran, I want to write a story about Kim."

A story about Kim? I pondered the significance of his proposal. Of course I knew it was a real tribute, but I figured he was probably just being courteous. After all, we had just met that morning. Nonetheless, I sensed Barry's sincerity and integrity and told him he was welcome to write away.

After meeting in Texas, Barry kept in touch with us, calling every few weeks. He had lots of questions and a heartfelt interest in Kim's life. We knew he was working on a screenplay with Kim as the central character, but I wasn't aware of any specifics or the status of the project. I trusted and respected him so I was not concerned. As excited as Kim and I were over the prospect of being involved with a Hollywood movie, I knew the chances of something ever materializing were slim.

Two years later, in the fall of 1986, Barry phoned from Los Angeles to tell us the exciting news: UA/MGM had just purchased his script about Kim! Dustin Hoffman, star of the popular films *Kramer vs. Kramer* (for which he won his first Academy Award for Best Actor), *Tootsie, Midnight Cowboy* and *The Graduate*, had signed on to star!

In an interview for a Swedish television program on Kim entitled *Verklighetens Rainman*, (2006), Barry recalled his experience of meeting Kim:

> I felt someone tap me on the shoulder and I turned around and right in my face was Rain Man. His name wasn't Rain Man then, it was Kim Peek. No one was talking to Kim, but I did, and within moments I recognized there was something very different going on in that large head. This was the first time that Kim had ever been in public where he engaged a person in a conversation. When I flew home, all the way on the airplane I kept thinking, "this is a character in search of a movie," and I felt like if I could

come up with a story, this character would be something no one has ever seen before.

Still, what was missing is, what launches the story? What's the twist? What's different? Then I thought I'm going to give him a brother. A brother he doesn't know he has. Two disconnected brothers—one unredeemed man and one unrealized human being—and it all comes together when their foreheads touch, none of those other things can compare to what humans are about… about touching and loving.

Our Trip to Hollywood

In November of 1986, a few days after Barry telephoned telling us the exciting news that UA/MGM had purchased his script about Kim, Dustin Hoffman's New York office phoned to verify that Dustin wanted to play the lead role and wished to meet with Kim at our home in Salt Lake City the following month.

Kim was thrilled and became obsessed with the idea of meeting Dustin Hoffman. He asked me numerous times every day when Dustin would be coming to visit, but the star's office had difficulty finding a date when he would be able to make the trip. Finally, we received word from Dustin's agency that he had been detained in Europe and would like for us to travel to Los Angeles to meet with him the following week. The airline tickets were bought and paid for and a room had been reserved for us at the Century Plaza in Beverly Hills. On February 5, 1986, Kim and I set off for the airport, excited about our journey to L.A.

We arrived at the airport about an hour before departure. Our stroll down the terminal to the boarding gate was evocative of the poster that was later designed to advertise *Rain Man* in movie theaters and magazines: Dustin and Tom (Cruise) walking down the roadway leading from Wallbrook, the institution where Raymond (Rain Man) had spent most of his life.

Little did we realize that our lives were on the cusp of becoming very, very different. The sunrises ahead of us would be filled with new places and new experiences, meeting hundreds of thousands of new people, and Kim would mature and grow in ways not thought possible.

When we arrived in L.A. we were greeted at the airport by Barry Morrow who literally leaped over to Kim when he spotted us, embracing him and saying how happy he was to see us. Barry, who remains a good friend of ours to this day, is like a breath of fresh air. He's a bundle of energy, animated in all his actions and his conversations.

"You're still that good man, Barry Morrow," Kim said in his booming voice. "Where do we go from here?"

Barry suggested we head downtown for lunch.

"To get to downtown, you need to take the airport exit onto La Cienga Blvd, Don't you?"

"Right… we'll take La Cienga as far as …"

Kim interrupted with: "To Hollywood and Sunset."

"And then you go up Sunset and the restaurant is right near Mann's Chinese Theater," said Barry.

Amazed at his knowledge of the roadways, Barry asked me whether we'd ever been to L.A.

"Once before, back in 1965," I said, "but he knows all the main roads, the freeway exits, most of the downtown streets, and the locations of nearly all businesses, movie theaters and ball parks. He also knows a lot of history about Los Angeles and the entire state of California. He will probably comment on many things as you drive along. Don't be surprised if he flips from subject to subject," I added.

It was an interesting ride into town. Kim knew every street and would advise Barry a few blocks in advance the names of specific streets that were coming up and how far it was to the exit we were looking for.

He also commented on many buildings and sites we passed.

"You know, Fran, I still can't believe this!" Barry exclaimed.

Barry glanced over at Kim who was repetitively shuffling his fingers in front of his face. "What do you see when you look at your fingers like that, Kim?" asked Barry.

"Lots of things you wonder about, Barry Morrow." And that was the extent of his answer.

We enjoyed a delicious lunch together, after which Barry announced he wanted to take us on one more detour before bringing us to our hotel.

Barry parked a few blocks away from the Sidewalk of the Stars and Mann's Chinese Theatre. We walked along the sidewalk, reading the names of stars, until we came upon a small photo shop tucked away behind several large poster displays of famous films. Barry directed us into the shop and suggested that the three of us have our photo taken as a souvenir for when we return home.

After posing for a picture all together, Barry had the photographer snap a photo of Kim by himself.

"We'll put your picture on a T-shirt and give it to Dustin in the morning. OK, Kim? And how about a warm-up shirt for me?" added Barry.

No sooner said than done. A larger-than-life-sized picture of Kim appeared on an oversized t-shirt.

"Dustin will know he's the real Rain Man when we give him this shirt, won't he?" smiled Kim.

At the hotel, we waved off the doorman and the bellman and carried our luggage over to the registration desk.

"Rain Man is here!" said Kim to the clerk.

"Yes, we have been expecting you," she smiled.

Barry escorted us to our room on the 22nd floor, which had a plaque on the door reading, "Presidential Suite." The bathroom was nearly as large as our living room at home—with two showers! There were two bathrobes laid out, a fully-stocked bar—everything! Barry told us to be ready bright and early the next morning, informing us that after our meeting with Dustin, the top-dogs at UA/MGM, who had heard so much about Kim from Barry, wanted to meet with us.

"Rest is important, Dad. Big day tomorrow. I'll have to ask Dustin about a couple of things in *Kramer vs. Kramer* that got him his 1980 Oscar. Remember, Dad? It won five big ones: Best Picture, Best Actor, Best Supporting Actress—Meryl Streep, Best Director, and Best Adapted Screenplay."

"And who directed *Kramer vs. Kramer*?" I asked.

"Robert Benton, a Stanley Jaffe production," he answered.

"Yes, I'm sure the two of you will have a lot to talk about," I replied.

After thumbing through several large telephone directories and a couple of brochures in the room, Kim leaned back on the bed and said, "Dad, would this ever have happened to you if I hadn't been born?"

"No, never. This is a special thing that is happening to a special person," I answered.

Two minutes later, Kim was snoring. His hands were covering his ears, but the peacefulness of his sleep told me that he was one happy guy. It is sometimes a bit hard to tell when Kim is enjoying something. There was no question about it this time.

We arose the next morning at about 6:00 a.m. It had been a relatively sleepless night for me, but Kim slept a solid seven hours. After we shaved and showered, I helped Kim get dressed. His mind was on a thousand different things, from meeting with Dustin to talking about movies, plays, operas and several things that were on our schedule when we returned to Salt Lake City.

At breakfast in the hotel coffee shop, several waiters stopped by to find out the day they were born and the day they would turn 65 and could retire. Kim also asked to know the towns they grew up in or had lived in so that he could tell them their local television stations and area codes.

Kim also spoke with the doorman and discovered that he had been on the Los Angeles Rams football team, but quit the same year Merlin Olsen from Utah State University had joined the team. The doorman had been in spring training with Merlin, so Kim told him about Merlin's years at USU in Logan, Utah, his days with the L.A. Rams, and several things about his family and his career.

"How does he know these things?" the doorman asked me.

"I wish I could explain it. He reads everything, every atlas, almanac, book, biography, magazine—if it has been printed, he has probably read it. That's a bit too much to believe, I guess, but that's how it is!" I answered.

"Every day," I said, "he spends at least three hours reading, learning and storing information, waiting to recall whatever he needs to know. Sometimes I tease him by calling him 'Kim-puter.' You can't believe these things about Kim unless you spend quite a bit of time paying close attention to him. Even then, it still seems impossible!"

A few minutes later, Barry picked us up and brought us to the MGM studio offices. When we got to the room where we were to meet Dustin, we were greeted at the door by an unfamiliar-looking man.

"You don't look like Dustin," said Kim.

The man introduced himself as Murray Schisgal.

"You wrote *Tootsie*. Jessica Lange got the 1982 Academy Award for Best Supporting Actress. Produced and Directed by Sydney Pollack. He's a friend of our friend, Robert Redford, who lives just south of us, at Sundance. I once helped William DeVane with his horses near Redford's place," said Kim.

"Yes, that's right," responded Schisgal.

"Fine film. Dustin deserved an Oscar for that one, too!"

Moments later, a rather small man wearing a denim jacket, canvas shoes and Levis approached us. Kim put his hands on the man's shoulders, touched his nose to the man's nose, and said, "Dustin Hoffman, from this moment we shall be as one."

Hoffman turned to me and skeptically asked me whether I had instructed Kim to say that.

"No," I answered. "I guess he's been thinking a lot about this special moment."

Dustin shook hands with Barry and me and we all moved into the room.

"Dustin," said Kim, "I've got a present for you!"

Kim handed Dustin the small bag containing the photo-printed t-shirt that had been made outside of Mann's Theater. Dustin opened it and held the shirt up for all to see. Everyone clapped and told Kim how great it looked. Dustin took off his jacket and laid it across his chair, stripped off his shirt and wiggled into the *Rain Man* t-shirt.

Kim Fran, Dustin Hoffman, and some of the RAIN MAN team

"How do I look, Kim?"

"You look just like me!" Kim said excitedly.

Dustin chuckled and then walked to the corner of the room and began dialing the telephone.

A tall bearded man in his early thirties approached Kim and introduced himself as Marty Brest.

"You did a fine job directing *Beverly Hills Cop,*" Kim said.

"Thank you. I'm very happy to meet you, Kim. I've been selected to direct *Rain Man.*"

"We'll get to work together a lot, won't we?" said Kim.

"I hope so," smiled Marty.

The next few hours with Dustin were like a dream. Dustin was eager to get to know Kim and see for himself some of Kim's remarkable abilities. He told Kim the birthdates of his wife and children and Kim instantaneously told him what day of the week they had been born on, what day their birthdays would fall on in the coming year, and what day of the week it would be when they turned 65.

Awestruck, Dustin asked me how Kim did it.

"Maybe someday we'll find out," I told him. "He won't share his computation techniques with anyone!"

Dustin proceeded to ask Kim an array of historical questions.

"Can you tell me about the battle of Bunker Hill?"

"Took place in Massachusetts on June 17, 1775 between the Americans and the British," said Kim.

"Do you know the day of the week?" I prodded him.

"It was a Saturday," he replied.

"In 1836, do you know who was president of the United States?" asked Dustin.

"James K. Polk was president. He was born in North Carolina in 1795 and died in Tennessee in 1849.

His vice president was George Dallas."

"Do you know where he was born?"

"In Pennsylvania."

As Kim paced back and forth along across the room, Dustin noticed he was twisting the small piece of venetian blind cord he always carries with him. I explained that the cord was like a security blanket for Kim. He frequently holds it up close to his face and twists it repeatedly. Dustin asked me whether I had an extra cord. Fortunately, I always carry a couple of extras and handed one to Dustin.

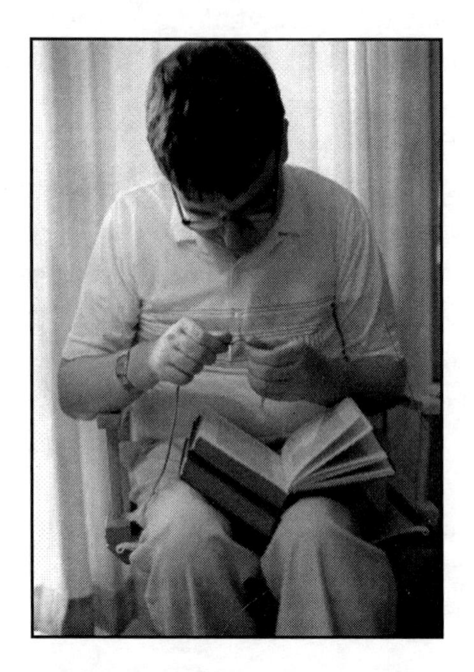

Dustin took the cord, knots on each end, and walked towards Kim. Kim didn't pay any attention to his approach. Then, for almost an hour, Dustin replicated every motion Kim made, including twisting the cord. On occasion, Kim would turn his head to watch Dustin moving about, but did nothing about it.

Others in the group asked Kim questions about British monarchs, baseball, football, boxing, horse racing, the Bible and a wide range of subjects. When someone asked him about Puccini, Kim hummed aloud a couple of bars from the composer's most famous pieces.

"You know, Puccini was born in Lucca, Italy, on December 22, 1858 and died in Brussels on November 12, 1924. His most popular operas are *La Boheme* and *Madame Butterfly*."

All the while Kim moved about the room, Dustin continued to shadow him. He wasn't mimicking Kim so much as trying to establish some basic behavioral patterns that he later incorporated into his character in the movie, Raymond.

At lunch break, I took Kim to find a restroom. We located it quickly and were surprised to find a sign on its door that read, "COLOR EMPLOYEES ONLY."

"Haven't they heard about the Civil Rights Act?" queried Kim. A young man standing at the restroom door explained, "You are in the production area where the movie *Colors* is being produced. Go ahead and use the restroom. It's okay."

Later that day, Dustin told us he wanted us to meet one of his friends. He took us down the hall and knocked on the door marked "Dennis Hopper." Kim immediately began to sing the theme from the movie *Easy Rider*. Dustin joined in and pushed the door open just as Hopper was about to turn the door handle.

Hearing the singing, Hopper joined in, putting his arm around Dustin's shoulder. Dustin extended his arm around Kim's waist and together the trio sang the theme song over and over.

"Dennis," said Dustin, "Meet Kim… the Real Rain Man!"

Taking Kim's hand, Hopper introduced himself and asked Kim how he knew the music from *Easy Rider.*

"My brother, Brian, and my sister, Ali, used to play it on our record player. Exciting movie. Came out in 1970."

Dustin prompted Hopper to tell Kim when he was born. Kim quickly reported that he had been born on a Tuesday, that his birthday this year would be on a Wednesday, and that it would be a Sunday when he turned 65. He then added, "You are a year older than Dustin. You look much younger than him, though."

Dustin looked down and shook his head a couple of times and cast a wry smile, raising his eyebrows and shrugging his shoulders.

We then returned to the studio where Dustin continued to incredulously quiz Kim. He asked Kim to name the books of the Old Testament, to which Kim asked, "Do you want to hear them frontwards or backwards?"

It took about two minutes for Kim to name them all (frontwards, as requested by Dustin). He included the New Testament as well.

"He hasn't logged all the scriptures verbatim," I said, "but if you ask him about certain passages, he can usually locate them for you and will often explain the main idea of the scripture."

"Does he read a lot, Fran?" asked Dustin.

"That's an understatement!" I replied. "Not only has he read over 8,000 books, he can recall nearly everything about every book he's ever read. He may also relate things he hears people say to what he's read. He reads all types of materials: historical books, literary novels, almanacs, catalogs, magazines, pamphlets, telephone books, encyclopedias. Once he's read a book at lightening-speed, the content is not only retained in his brain, but it seems to be filed away in association-banks for immediate recall."

"No one so far has been able to figure out how he does it," I explained. "His brain is so complex that it continues to mystify everyone who spends any appreciable amount of time talking with him."

Barry left the room and returned with two volumes of Reader's Digest condensed books, each containing four or five condensed books. Barry opened one book to the contents page and said, "Kim, I'm looking at *The Nun's Story*. What can you tell me about it?"

"First book in the Volume 4, 1956 edition. Written by Kathryn Hulme. Other books in that 1956 edition are: *Merry Christmas, Mr. Baxter* by Edward Streeter; *The Success* by Helen Howe; *The Diamond Hitch* by Frank O'Rourke; and *The Sleeping Partner* by Winston Graham," concluded Kim.

"Barry, did you bring those books to the studio?" asked Dustin, a little doubtful that maybe

Kim and Barry had rehearsed this mind-blowing display.

"No! I noticed them in the reception room in the bookcase behind the secretary's desk when we came in. Kim did this in Texas when I first met him. Then, when he came to my home, he told me about the books in several of the editions I have," said Barry.

Dustin pulled up a chair from the desk across the room, moved it to the front of the group sitting on the sofa, sat down and confided to us that when he had first read Barry's script he had assumed it was a stroke of creative genius, because surely there was no way any person could do the things described.

Kim Fran, Dustin Hoffman, and Marty Brest

"I had to fictionalize several of the events, but Kim is presented just as he is," said Barry. "When I met him back in 1984, I couldn't believe it either! Since then, he has accumulated even more knowledge," exclaimed Barry.

The day flew by and in what seemed like no time at all Dustin needed to be on his way to his next appointment. Before excusing himself and saying his goodbyes, he arose from his chair, walked towards Kim, extended his arms and pulled him upright. "Kim, when you met me this morning you said, 'from this moment on, we shall be as one.' I would like to say something to you, too: I may be the star, but you are the heavens."

Dustin and Kim touched noses as they embraced. Dustin's moist eyes remained focused on Kim's face for several seconds. He wiped his eyes with the back of his hand, then turned and shook hands with Barry and me. Placing both of his hands around mine, he thanked me for bringing Kim to meet him and told me that he might be in touch in the next few weeks as he prepared for the role.

He walked over to the other people in the room and shook their hands. With his briefcase under his arm, he once again walked over to Kim and embraced him tightly.

"See ya', Rain Man."

"Dustin, be the good man that you are!" said Kim.

Neither Kim nor I will ever forget that special day with Dustin. It was an exceptional treat for me to meet a celebrity who I had seen in several movies and who proved to be as extraordinary a person as he was an actor. Yet to Kim, Dustin was primarily a new and very special friend, forever.

"Dustin is a great man. He will be remembered for many movies and stage appearances, but mostly, he will be thought of for being Rain Man," concluded Kim.

Over the next couple of years, the road to the development of the movie *Rain Man* was a rocky one. Marty Brest, who was originally going to direct the film, left the scene. The studio tried to solicit the directorship of Stephen Spielberg and Sydney Pollack, but to no avail. Finally, Barry Levinson signed on to direct the movie. Together with Dustin Hoffman and Barry Morrow, they demonstrated sufficient amount of determination to make *Rain Man* a reality.

Ron Bass was brought onboard to revise and rewrite the script with Morrow. A hot young actor, Tom Cruise, signed on to co-star. Originally Cruise wanted to play the part of Raymond, the savant, but Dustin felt strongly about playing that part and ultimately it was agreed that Cruise would portray Raymond's brother, Charlie. The persistence and creative talents of Morrow, Hoffman, Cruise, and Levinson ultimately brought the project to fruition.

Kim turned out to be too complex a character for the story. Hoffman is a very thorough actor who painstakingly prepares for all his roles. Throughout his research for *Rain Man,* Dustin met several autistic savants who characteristically demonstrated a frustrating inability to communicate and share their feelings. From his experiences working with the savants he selected to study, including Kim, Dustin ultimately developed the composite character of Raymond Babbitt.

During the production of the film, Dustin got Kim a black leather *Rain Man* jacket, which Barry Morrow presented to Kim at the New Mexico State Arc convention in Albuquerque prior to the release of the movie. Dustin also sent us several autographed posters and a director's chair signed by himself, Tom Cruise, and members of the production crew.

Kim and I were invited by Dustin to attend the premier of *Rain Man* in Hollywood and to the reception that followed. Kim sat through the showing but did not seem to "watch" the movie; rather, he kept his eyes focused downward on his lap and remained immersed in his own world. When Barry, who was seated next to Kim and had noticed his preoccupation, asked Kim if he had watched the movie, Kim said, "I watched it with my heart!"

I don't think that Kim ever really made an emotional connection to the movie but, on occasion, he does still blurt out his favorite line in the movie, "I buy my underwear at K-Mart!"

Everyone was thrilled and amazed when *Rain Man* opened in theaters and earned rave reviews, drawing impressive crowds and commanding a strong box office. There had been some concern that there might not be a lot of interest in or appreciation for a drama such as this, but such concern proved unfounded. *Rain Man* was nominated for eight Academy Awards, more than any of us had dared hope for!

Kim and I were invited to several pre-Academy Awards events and on the night of the ceremony we attended a special party in Los Angeles, hosted by Barry Morrow's sister, where we watched the televised broadcast of the Academy Awards. The excitement was indescribable as *Rain Man* racked up the four major Academy Awards that year: Best Picture, Best Actor, Best Director and Best Screen Play. As Dustin accepted his Oscar for Best Actor, the first thing he said was, "My special thanks to Kim Peek for his help in making *Rain Man* a reality." I couldn't help but shed a tear.

Kim and I were thrilled for Dustin and honored to have been mentioned by name at the Academy Awards! Dustin did a remarkable job of portraying Raymond Babbitt in the movie and was entirely deserving of the Best Actor award. Unfortunately, we have heard that after *Rain Man* Dustin struggled with being stereotyped as a result of his portrayal being so convincing. He has thus distanced himself from any public association with Kim in the years since the movie. Nonetheless, Kim and I remain two of Dustin Hoffman's biggest fans. He is one of the greatest actors and greatest people ever.

We owe both Barry and Dustin a very profound debt of gratitude. Before parting with them in L.A. on that memorable day when Dustin first met Kim, Dustin took me aside and, with great earnestness, told me that more people needed to meet and know Kim, and he urged me to take Kim out of his sheltered world and share my son with others. Barry concurred. Since then, it's been quite a ride.

Kim with Barry Morrow

CHAPTER 5
Kim's Debut

After *Rain Man* won its four Academy Awards, Kim suddenly became a celebrity, first locally, then internationally. From the moment Dustin spoke the name Kim Peek at the Academy Awards, the phones started ringing off the hook as the press sought to learn about the "Real Rain Man."

At first I was very leery of all the media attention and was inclined to protect Kim by keeping him out of the limelight. I was also very reluctant to accept invitations from organizations that requested he appear as a featured guest. Throughout his life Kim had been sheltered and protected. He had not learned and was not expected to be able to learn how to interact with individuals or groups of people.

As a father, my first instinct was to protect my son and not subject him to the unfamiliar and often judgmental wider world. However, Barry Morrow and Dustin Hoffman's words continued to resonate in my mind: the world needs to know Kim.

I spent many hours soul-searching and thinking about the potential—good and bad—that might face us. In particular, I wondered what would happen if Kim were to interact with large groups of students and adults. Although not all of our family members agreed with my decision, I felt strongly that I had to take Kim out of his closeted, protected world and expose him to the sunshine and danger of the big, real world. It was time for Kim to make his debut!

I didn't want to force Kim into any situations where he would be uncomfortable, but I felt that I had to give him a chance to interact with people. I had to see if he wanted to meet and share his unique talents with others. I had to give him the opportunity to build a new life in an environment filled with all kinds of people and unknown challenges.

It was also very important to me that Kim would not be viewed as being exploited, so I ventured out slowly and cautiously. I initially decided to ask only for expenses and accepted no fees for Kim's appearances, hoping that would eliminate the prospect of people questioning my motives (more recently, in response to increased financial pressure, I accept a modest honorarium for our presentations). I would be alongside him at all times, not just to protect him from comments or any other kinds of confrontations, but also to help him interact with those who wished to meet him. I was scared to death that I would have a sideshow of a person who had mental retardation, and I could not allow that, but I reminded myself that if it did not work out, I could always find other ways of allowing Kim to be healthy, happy and able to pursue his unique talents.

At first, I was very nervous when we made presentations. I didn't know what Kim was going to say, how he was going to act, or what people would think of him and say to him. I was very concerned about things that might be said of him and to him by people who were uneducated in understanding differences in others; but I vowed that if that happened, I would not allow myself to get angry and would instead try to educate the person. I prayed that I was making the right decision for my son and that sharing him with the world would be of benefit to him and others. I could never have dreamed just how beneficial it would turn out to be!

Nothing in my life has been more positive and more fulfilling than to watch Kim mature and have others see him for who he truly is: a unique, loving, totally innocent and honest human being. He is the brightest, warmest, most amazing person I have ever known.

Interacting with groups and being exposed to different environments has allowed Kim to truly blossom. Once again he defied all odds and progressed in ways that he was never expected to. Much to the surprise and amazement of everyone, once he started interacting with others, going new places and trying new things, Kim underwent a near-miraculous transformation.

Those who had suspected Kim to be autistic told us that he would never develop social skills; that he would remain introverted, lacking a sense of humor and unable to develop feelings for others. Yet, in the past few years, the man who used to shy away from others and who would not so much as make eye contact with another person was delighting in the company of others, greeting friends and strangers alike with warm hugs and handshakes. It's almost as if he's been reborn.

Our good friend and expert on Savant Syndrome, Dr. Treffert, has recognized that Kim's positive reaction to interacting with others is not

Kim, Dr. Treffert, and Fran, 2006

unique; rather, it is quite "normal." In *Extraordinary People*, Treffert explains that, just like anyone else, savants love applause and positive feedback. "All of us enjoy doing that which we do well. Aside from any personal satisfaction our skills bring, the approval we get from others is important and acts as reinforcement and motivation to do even better" (p. 182).

Twenty five years ago I would have never dreamed Kim would become the person he is today. No one ever anticipated he would make the kind of progress he has. When I observe him interacting with groups and individuals, I think back to the first half of his life and am overwhelmed with pride and joy at how far he has come.

Although we had started presenting to school groups and organizations in the late 80's, the publication of my first book, *The Real Rain Man*, in 1996 led to even more requests for speaking engagements and school visits. Kim and I, by this time, had developed some comfortable routines and structure with our traveling. Although it was sometimes tiring, we found our interactions with the public at large to be both interesting and exhilarating.

To my amazement, once we started including book signings as part of our program, I noticed Kim's interpersonal skills improve even more. Today we bring copies of the book to most of our presentations so that anyone in the audience who wishes to buy a copy may do so on the spot. Kim and I then make ourselves available for autographs.

The scenario is usually the same: after we talk to a group and engage in a question-and-answer period,

Kim and I sit together at a table and people form a line for our signatures. Usually I sign first and then hand the book to Kim who very proudly and with much precision prints his name (using his left hand) and the date.

However, these "book signings" are never quite as simple or fast as one might expect. Generally, people want to engage Kim. The easiest and most effective way for them to do so is by telling him their dates of birth so that Kim can calculate the day of the week they were born, the day of the week their birthday will fall on in the current year, and the day and year they will turn 65. The incredulous response of the autograph seekers continues to delight and amaze me and keeps me from taking Kim's savant ability for granted.

Over the past few months we have been signing an increasing number of books, as the television documentaries, particularly *The Real Rain Man* that aired on The Discovery Channel here in the United States, have made Kim more popular.

Kim and I were honored to be invited to the 2007 Council for Exceptional Children Convention and Expo in Louisville, KY this Spring. We presented to an overflow crowd of very passionate educators who formed long lines to have their books signed and meet Kim. I was struck by the excitement with which the attendees waited in line, not just for the signature but also to have their pictures taken with Kim, me…and, of course, Oscar.

I am hoping that this new book will have a still greater appeal as it reflects even more clearly who Kim really is and demonstrates that it is not only his unmatched abilities that affect people, but also his kindness and commitment to making a difference in the lives of others.

Perhaps more than anyone else, I feel like Barry Morrow is very much responsible for Kim's new and improved, richer and fuller life. Barry remains a very important and beloved person in our lives and continues to support and celebrate Kim. Unfortunately, we do not get the opportunity to visit with him very often, but when we do it's like reconnecting with family.

Over the years, Barry has been most generous and cooperative, sharing his memories and perspectives on Kim with various interviewers, even contributing a preface to a previous book I wrote about Kim. His words poignantly capture the remarkable nature of Kim's transformation and testify to his profound impact on the lives of others:

> When I first met Kim, he touched me on the shoulder and told me so many things about myself—my phone number, for instance, all about my hometown, and all the television programs I had been involved in. But more than that, he told me to "think about myself." It's a challenge that I've continued to try to do. At the same time I've continued to think about Kim and what was formerly the kind of confined world that he lived in, a sort of prison that was created by the fact that he was unable to really venture out into the world. He loved his many books and shared the lives of the people and characters who lived within their covers.
>
> And while he has now been able to bring that world out to many people by lecturing to and

interacting with tens of thousands of people, especially children and young people around the country, a curious thing has happened to Kim: the bars of his prison have begun to fall aside and out has emerged not just a marvelously gifted human being, but a warm, compassionate, caring person who defies the labels of "autism" and "mental retardation."

In the past few years, since the movie "Rain Man" received its four Oscars in March 1989, Kim has become not only an outstanding role model for persons with disabilities, but a sign of hope to parents and families and a true inspiration to me and to countless others. I don't think anybody could spend five minutes with Kim and not come away with a slightly altered view of themselves, the world, and our potential as human beings.

I say to you, Kim, my dear and special friend, that watching your growth, your journey through life, and watching you, Fran, who is always there to guide him and to stand in the shadows when necessary to allow Kim to have the limelight for himself, is a wonderful testament to love, to our infinite capacity to grow, as well as to the extraordinary, unknown boundaries of our own minds and what we might do with Kim's unique example. (Peek, F., 1996, pp. xii-xiii)

CHAPTER 6
Spreading the Message

To date, Kim has interacted with over 3.5 million people! He is happy to talk to most anyone, but he especially enjoys meeting with groups of students at schools. By the time we arrive for a visit, the kids have learned a little bit about Kim and they usually have prepared lots of questions to ask him to see how much he really knows. Even though they have been told about Kim's amazing memory in fifteen areas, they are surprised and even disbelieving when

Kim and Fran, Bennion Jr. High School, 2006

they finally meet him. In fact, when we first started visiting schools in the late 1980's, a few students at one of the schools we visited thought that Kim had been tipped off to the questions and rehearsed all the answers. To prove them wrong, the school's principal took the students into her office with Kim and let them ask him all kinds of questions. That ended the skepticism! The students became believers and had no more doubts about the authenticity of his knowledge.

Kim answering student questions, 2006

Far from the introverted, withdrawn child he had been, today Kim is a very loving, affectionate person. Sometimes when we visit schools he will walk up to the students and want to hug them, put his hands on their shoulders, or touch their hands. As long as people understand Kim's limitations, they generally don't feel threatened; in fact, they find his gentle and affectionate nature to be heartwarming. On the other hand, when Kim behaves this way with adults and people who don't know him (as he frequently does when we're out in public), he can make others very uncomfortable.

I have tried to explain to Kim that it is not appropriate to touch and embrace strangers or get very close up in their faces, but that is one of the social skills Kim has not been able to grasp. He certainly does not mean to be threatening, and therefore he cannot conceive of why anyone would feel frightened or intimidated by his gestures of kindness. Knowing Kim as I do, I myself sometimes forget that his behaviors might be bothersome to others—until I catch him in an airport or hotel lobby getting too-close-for-comfort with an unsuspecting bystander and see the fear or confusion in that person's eyes. When this happens, I gently separate Kim from the other person and, introducing him as the "Real Rain Man," ask the person to tell us his or her birth date so that Kim can impress with his lightning calendar calculations, thereby revealing his incredible savant ability. This helps the other person understand that Kim is unique and harmless while at the same time allowing Kim to feel a sense of pride rather than shame.

Interacting with someone as unique as Kim shows students that it's okay to be different. By spending time with Kim, they learn to become more comfortable around people who are outside of the norm. It has been incredibly gratifying for me to see the impact Kim has on most everyone he meets, not just people living with or caring for those with disabilities. Students, seniors, people of every culture are awed by Kim's uncanny wealth of knowledge and are won over by his pleasant, wholesome, totally honest and innocent personality.

Because it is Kim's savant skills that initially intrigue an audience, I preface our presentations with a short discussion about how the normal brain functions and contrast that with an explanation of how Kim's brain works. Sometimes I use the analogy that Kim's brain has no waste basket the way a normal brain or even a computer does. Instead of filtering out things that he may not want to remember or may not be interested in, he retains everything he takes in.

After introducing Kim in this way, we move on to "the message," which has become the hallmark of our presentations. Remaining true to my commitment not to exploit Kim or just focus on his uniqueness without context, I explain to the group that Kim wants to be remembered for more than just what he knows; even more importantly, he wants everyone, especially young people, to learn from him that each of us is different and special, and that we all deserve to be treated in line with the Golden Rule of "do unto others." In Kim's own words: "Learn to recognize and respect differences in others, treat them as you want them to treat you so we can have a better world to live in. Care, share and be your best! And you don't have to be handicapped to be different. Everybody's different."

This message is very simple yet powerful. It says, all you've got to do is remember to treat other people like you want them to treat you. Recently, this message has become even more relevant with the movement towards inclusion of students with disabilities and the implementation of character education programs. Schools and the larger community are becoming increasingly diverse and there is greater demand than ever for Kim to talk to school groups about recognizing and respecting differences. We keep a very busy travel schedule, yet there are often times when I have to refuse invitations for speaking engagements because we simply do not have the time for all the requests that we get.

Sometimes when we accept speaking engagements the presentations are opened up to the general public. Such was the case on a cold Sunday afternoon at a school in North Dakota, when a gentleman who had come to hear Kim speak introduced himself as the president of National Professional Resources, Inc., a small but nationally known video production company located in NY. After a brief conversation, he proposed that we collaborate with him on a video that would address the value of recognizing and celebrating differences in others. He excitedly talked about how a product such as this could be distributed to schools and community groups, thus allowing Kim's message to be shared in a much more expansive way. He easily sold me on the idea. Once again, Kim was to be the subject of a video production—but this one was to be different. It was to focus primarily on Kim's message for students, parents and educators, rather than on scientific or medical issues.

Two months later, a film crew and contingent of staff from National Professional Resources met us in Salt Lake City. We had three stops on our itinerary for the taping that day: Bennion Junior High School, the Salt Lake City Public Library, and a small but comfortable conference space for interviews. Initially, the process of taping wasn't much different from what we were used to. As usual, we were asked questions about Kim's brain and his awesome gifts—but then there was a twist. The questions started to include exciting concepts that Kim and I have always focused upon, such as respect and responsibility, thereby segueing into the realm of character education and social-emotional learning. The producer wanted to explore questions such as how we could help students become more aware of the significance of positive behavior and personal attributes; how we could help promote an understanding of differences within schools; how we could help students with disabilities become more valued for their uniqueness and appreciated for their strengths, even if they looked, sounded, or acted differently; and how we could convey the need for students to develop and display emotionally sensitive and empathetic characteristics.

Fran, Kim, and staff of National Professional Resources, Inc.

It was an exciting day for both of us. We felt positive when it was over, however we had become so accustomed to being filmed over the years that we did not give the project much thought after the crew left. Then, in early October, 2006, Kim and I were scheduled to speak to the New York State Council of Exceptional Children (NYSCEC) in Albany and were told that we would have the opportunity to see the "premier" of the DVD by National Professional Resources entitled, *Celebrating Diversity: A Universal Message from the Real Rain Man* (2007).

We arrived in Albany and were escorted to the hotel where we were treated to a showing of this video. Kim does not usually watch programs about himself, and this was no exception. But I was thoroughly captivated. The final product was extremely impressive and truly conveys our message in a unique and powerful way. It presents quite clearly the need to increase acceptance, foster respect for others and understand differences, while also addressing the need to promote tolerance, develop appreciation of others and inspire caring. The only part of the trip that was more exciting was when the organizers of the conference had a surprise birthday party, including a huge, delicious cake, to celebrate Kim's 57th birthday. In all my years of observing Kim at his birthday parties, this is the first time he has ever successfully blown out the candles!

Since that time, we have been informed

that *Celebrating Diversity* has been honored with a Silver Telly Award. For over a quarter century the Telly Awards have honored the very best local, regional, and cable television commercials and programs, as well as the finest video and film productions. The 27th Annual Telly Awards, which recognized *Celebrating Diversity*, received over 13,000 entries from all 50 states and 5 continents. The Silver Telly is the highest honor and is one of the most sought after awards by industry leaders.

We are very proud of all the awards with which we have been honored, but there is one award that stands out among them all. Today, whenever we make an appearance, we bring along this very popular prop… the Oscar statuette. People love to hold the famous gold-plated statuette and have their pictures taken with Kim and the award. Kim loves to share this memento with others, and after doing so for the past several years, some 250,000 people have held the Oscar, causing the gold finish to wear off in places. However, we don't mind that good old Oscar is a little worse for the wear—on the contrary, we are proud to be able to share it with people. I would wager that ours is indeed the most loved Oscar of all time. Rather than sitting on a shelf collecting dust, it is admired by more people than probably any other statue ever won.

Of course, the Motion Picture Academy confers no award for Best Inspiration for a Film, so Kim himself never received an award. However, when we visited Barry Morrow in California two years after he was presented with the statuette for Best Screen Play, we returned home with quite a souvenir: Barry's own cherished Oscar!

Never in our wildest dreams did we expect to return from our visit to California with Barry's well-deserved award. We were just honored to have been a part of the film and were excited to be visiting our dear friend. He had moved into new offices just north of his home in Claremont and invited us to see them.

Several awards were displayed on his walls, and shelves of books and trophies highlighted the main room. High on one of the shelves glistened the golden Oscar. We hadn't seen it since the morning after that night in March of 1989 when we stopped by Barry's home to meet several media people and congratulate Barry personally for his great success.

Barry reached up to the statue and gently lifted it down. He held it at arm's length and I could see his eyes dance as his thoughts reflected back on that special evening two years earlier.

"Beautiful, isn't it?" he said. "I wouldn't have it if it weren't for you, Kim. It belongs to both of us. I want to share it with you. OK?"

"You can't do that, Barry," I spoke up. "It is such an important monument to your talents and your success. It needs to be near you and your friends."

"No, I really want Kim to take it home with him. Enjoy it. Share it with your friends, too," insisted Barry.

He placed it in a specially-made carrying bag and handed it to me. Then he hugged me very emotionally and I returned the feelings. Finally, he approached Kim, put his arms tightly around him and said, "We are a great team!"

"Together we are forever, Barry," said Kim as he tilted his head to one side and then turned away. We talked more with Barry about our having the Oscar and what we might do with it back in Salt Lake.

"Share it with people, just like you are sharing Kim with them," said Barry.

Bottom of Oscar

Clearly, the best way to share both Kim and the Oscar with others is through our personal visits and group presentations. Anyone who meets Kim realizes that he is one of the most unique and "different" individuals a person could ever encounter! To see him across a room or on the street it would be easy to misjudge him. You might assume he was dangerous or crazy, making loud noises and pacing about. Or, you might think he was simply mentally retarded and lacked any intelligence at all. Of course, these assumptions could not be further from the truth!

Ann Ricks, a teacher at Bennion Junior High School in Salt Lake City, has been inviting Kim to meet with her students for 12 years. She was recently interviewed for *Celebrating Diversity* (2007) and spoke about the impact that Kim has on these students:

> When Kim's visit is first announced, sometimes the kids are a little nervous or hesitant because they haven't been around people like him. But as soon as Kim walks into the classroom they are just amazed and fascinated by him. They absolutely love him… Sometimes he will walk up to the students and hug them or touch their hands—he's a very loving person, which is great for the kids because it helps put them at ease. Once they see him, they see he's not as scary as they think he might be, and once they get to know Kim it helps them be more comfortable with kids who are not just like they are.

Kim with Ann Ricks

New York

Dr. Mary Rhodes, the school's principal, welcomes Kim's twice-annual visits to Bennion Jr. High School:

> We find the relevance and the impact of Kim's visits to be extraordinary. We are relating Kim to some of our character education lessons, emphasizing the importance of emotional intelligence and preparing students to work in the workplace with all kinds of individuals.... Our school participates in the national program, Community of Caring, which embraces five core values, including respect and responsibility. Respect means respecting everyone, and we have a responsibility to get along with others. Kim's visits help promote empathy and the kind of characteristics that are going to allow students to get along with each other. This also helps promote inclusion.

I am always moved by the letters and expressions of gratitude we receive. The following are statements from some of the students who have interacted with Kim:

> I was really excited to meet both Kim and Fran Peek. Some of the things that impressed me about Kim were the fact that he was just so kind and so nice, and that he has changed so much from how he used to be. We watched a film about him and we saw that he was a very non-touchy, non-emotional type of person; but yet, then again, you come and meet him and

he's very different and he's very touchy, very feely, very nice and very sweet. [Andrea R., student]

Kim has a great deal of respect for everybody. It really amazed me, actually, his compassion for everybody and the respect that he has. Somebody who is caring… I really enjoyed that about him. Now, seeing Kim and meeting him has changed my thoughts and opinions about people with disabilities. [Amanda C., student]

Over the years, many educators and parents of children with disabilities have spoken and written to me, telling me how inspiring it was for them to hear from Kim.

It was a remarkable experience to meet Kim. He's an inspiration to everybody who meets him, in two different ways: one is that we're able to be more aware of people who have disabilities and people who have advantages, and be able to see that we're actually all different… and the way we learn and process information is just different for everyone. I think his message is very strong and clear in that regard…. I think this is something people really need to learn. I believe it's important for teachers to know that if children don't learn the way they teach, then they must start finding out the way children process information and their learning style preferences and start teaching that way. (Marjorie S., Educator)

The reason I came to meet Kim is because I know he has a lot to offer. And I want people to become educated about what people with disabilities can do, what they can offer people. These people with disabilities have big hearts; they have a lot to give. I have a child of my own who has disabilities and it breaks your heart when others don't understand. They can be very cruel. But once they learn what these kids have to offer, they become more accepting of them. My little girl probably has the biggest, most loving heart you'll ever see. Generous. She's always thinking of others. To look at her I think you'd be a little nervous… People are afraid. People need to become educated. They need to know how to handle her and include her and respect her. People are mean to her but she is just blissfully happy. In her world there is no such thing as strangers, just friends that she hasn't met yet. (Linda F., parent)

Over the past two decades we have also been presenting to business and civic/community groups throughout the country and in Canada, ranging from Rotary to Border Patrol and everything in between. We also frequently present to church groups. What follows is an excerpt from a letter I received in early 2007 by Roger Van Lieshoot from the Business Leadership Network.

> Your message of full inclusion and valuing differences continues to resonate, and like a fine wine you get better and better every time I hear you speak. You are a father and son team that is without equal and the hardest working and most dedicated volunteers serving the disability community. I am so proud and honored to have had the privilege to share time with you, and grateful for the generosity, kindness and leadership you give so freely.

CHAPTER 7
Advocacy and Advice

Since Kim's childhood, much has changed and improved in the way children with disabilities are educated, treated and accepted. I am proud to have devoted much time and effort to affecting such changes and reforming disability law and policy.

Throughout my lifetime I have volunteered with a variety of organizations focusing on the needs of and programs for people with disabilities and their families. My volunteer activities have included leadership roles with parent groups as well as education and medical associations. As part of my involvement in legislative activities, I worked with Utah governors and three U.S. presidents, advocating for people with disabilities, even helping draft education law for Utah that became a model for Public Law 94-142, The Education Act for All Children, passed by the U.S. Congress in 1974. I was most privileged to serve as Utah's Primary Hearing Officer for Public Law 94-142, and have worked with teachers and parents in understanding and implementing

Individual Education Programs (IEP) for youth with disabilities as they were mainstreamed into public schools. I am past president of the Utah Easter Seal Society and the Utah Association for Retarded Citizens (the Arc) and served on the board of the Salt Lake City United Way.

Over the past several years, Kim and I have been honored by numerous civic and volunteer organizations for our endeavors to promote acceptance of individuals with disabilities. In 1987 I was honored with the "Don Quixote Award," the Arc of Utah's highest honor. In 1988 I was selected Western Region Volunteer of the Year by the National Arc. Also in 1988, I was named International Parent of the Year by TASH, an organization of professionals serving persons with severe handicaps.

In April of 1989, the Utah State Board of Education presented Kim with his High School graduation diploma. Three years later the Utah State University College of Education honored both Kim and me. Kim was also selected as USU's Honorary Valedictorian and Outstanding Student of their College of Education for the year 1992, while I was saluted as Outstanding Parent/Mentor and Teacher. The school presented us with plaques honoring us as individuals who were "Devoting Their Lives to Humane Understanding." Several organizations that have hosted Kim have presented similar awards. In 1997, Kim and I were recognized by the National Arc for our nationwide communication efforts, teaching more than 2.7 million people that "disabled doesn't mean unable."

When the Winter Olympics were held in Salt Lake City in 2002, Kim was invited by Mayor Rocky Anderson to meet and talk with many of the athletes and the representatives that accompanied them. Soon after hosting the Winter Olympics, Salt Lake City hosted the Paralympics. Kim and I were honored to be selected to carry a torch in the Paralympics Parade. Together with Kim's brother, Brian, and sister, Alison, the crowds cheered us along the route to the stadium. The special torch Kim carried stands in our living room today, along with many other awards and mementos he has received, including the bronze medal and the Sportsman medal he won at the first Utah Special Olympics in 1970 at the University of Utah.

Kim with New Ability Award

At the New Ability Award Gala in Fall of 2004, Kim and I received the New Freedom Foundation's Transformational New Ability Award, as presented by the World Ability Federation. We were only the second recipients of this award. The first was Christopher Reeve. We were happy to be able to use this platform to share our message of hope and determination: Live life, whatever your circumstances, to the fullest. Use your abilities rather than focusing on things in life that you cannot do. This is what makes for an extraordinary life.

I believe that our efforts on behalf of serving students with special needs have made a difference. Today, more and more students with special needs are included in the regular classroom, and educators are better trained in how to work with such students. But ongoing effort from parents is essential. I am proud to inspire parents I meet to become involved in advocacy work.

I am often asked, both in person and by mail or at interviews, what advice I would give to other parents of children with disabilities. My first question is always, "Do you belong to your parent group?" I continue to be amazed *at* how many do not. I offer parents the names of three or four parent groups that can they can go to and I encourage them to become members. It's important for parents to realize they're not the only ones in the world who have a child with autism or some other kind of disability. The support and understanding that these groups offer parents is invaluable.

As more and more parent groups form and the size of groups increases, there is a greater opportunity for parents to work together to advocate for children with special needs. Today, many groups have the capacity and collective influence to move the legislatures in terms of law, policy and practice.

I know that it is impossible to walk in another parent's shoes because each child and each family is so different, but I do think there are a few very general principles that are of critical importance and I offer parents the following advice: Continue to challenge your child, in spite of what may seem like insurmountable disabilities; don't accept the idea of an immovable plateau but rather provide as many opportunities as possible for your child, even if they seem outlandish.

The most important advice I can give to parents sounds quite simple, but really nothing really is more difficult: Realize that you are the parent of a child who is very much a human being with potential, just like every other child. He or she needs to be respected and loved. Don't raise your voice when your child needs your help. Be a bit more patient than you are with other children. Don't be embarrassed about taking your child out to stores, parties, and church. Children with disabilities need to become part of the regular community. As Kim frequently says, it is important to recognize and respect their differences, constantly reminding them how special they are, how much they are loved.

My heart goes out to other parents of special needs children. I am always happy to lend a sympathetic ear and offer suggestions. Parents of children with disabilities have a unique bond and I feel privileged to share experience, strength, and hope with them.

I am humbled and proud to hear from parents who share with me that not only are they inspired by Kim, but that they find inspiration in my story, as well. I have amassed a small collection of correspondences and have been moved by parent testimonials that have been recorded and shared with me. I am honored to present one of these in the hope that they will demonstrate how powerfully one parent can impact another.

> Kim's an exceptional human being, as is his father. I can just imagine what Fran must have gone though when Kim was growing up, before there was understanding about disabilities. I have two young children who were diagnosed at a year and a half with autism and it's been rough, but it makes me appreciate that today there is more of an understanding about autism and we know the proper steps necessary to help children with ASD. It's remarkable that Fran and Kim can stand in front of a group today and show people that it is possible to live a productive and happy, fulfilling life even with disabilities. That's what it's all about.
>
> I was devastated to find out about my children. It's not something that you think of when you want to have children, that they might have any kind of a disability let alone maybe never be able to speak, which is something that we have to face as parents, or be able to live indepen-dently or be a part of their community.
>
> Kim and Fran are an inspiration to us as parents. If they have been able to accomplish so much and overcome so much with the limited resources that they had back in the time Kim was a child...there's so much more available today and there's no excuse for parents and professionals today not to strive and advocate for kids with disabilities, and there's no excuse for the community around them to not be accepting of living and learning side by side and just be one as a community.

> I thought that today the opportunity to meet both of them was amazing, it really was. (Bob H., parent)

As a parent, one of the most gratifying comments I have read comes from Dr. Treffert. In a second edition of *Extraordinary People,* Treffert updates the reader on some of his impressions that have changed over the years of working with savants, and also restates two key impressions that have not changed since the book was originally published.

The first impression that has not changed is "the powerful, positive force of 'training the talent' can have in the savant to enhance the 'conduit toward normalization' with increased language acquisition, social abilities and daily living" (p. 384). Certainly, the most recent chapter of Kim's life story (post-*Rain Man*) supports this hypothesis.

The other impression that has not changed for Treffert over the years is heartwarming and reassuring to me and all those who care for savants, or any children with disabilities:

> Second [impression] is the awe-inspiring powerful, positive force that the love, dedication and determination of families, caretakers, teachers and others who not only care for the savant but care about him or her as well, can have on the savant by first recognizing, then reinforcing, and then finally celebrating ability rather than dis-ability... Whatever questions of a scientific nature might be

answered by looking at the savant, they are equaled or excelled by lessons in caring, belief, determination, appreciation, acceptance and unconditional positive regard that the savant and their families can teach us (p. 384).

CHAPTER 8
Labels are for Jars

A few years after Kim started interacting with people and exhibiting new interpersonal skills, he was reevaluated by the UCLA Center for Autism. Based on this evaluation, Dr. Peter Tanquay, the director of the program, told me that Kim's social skills were developing so fast that he believed Kim could not be labeled autistic. Instead, Kim was given the label of "prodigious intellectual memory savant." We have come to realize that labels are insignificant and never tell the whole story unless, that is, they are attached to jars.

Before *Rain Man*, Kim had autistic characteristics that are common among savants, such as never looking people in the eye and seemingly not registering emotion or revealing much personality. However, by the time he was reevaluated he had become eager to interact with others and easily engaged new people he met in conversation, usually by asking them their birth dates and home towns.

Kim has a very unusual way of expressing his feelings about people. He says he loves everybody, but one of the problems he has with many people is that he loves them momentarily and wants to talk to them, but then will abruptly walk away from them. He may initially be interested in someone because that person "has white hair like my neighbor," but unless someone shows a sustained interest in him, he quickly loses interest himself. The people Kim comes to care for the most are people who give him attention and put their arms around him or hold his hand, showing that they have a sustained interest rather than just looking at him and walking past.

Kim and Melissa Knoll, 2006

The strongest emotions Kim exhibits are triggered by things he reads about rather than person to person contact or direct experience. For example, when Kim reads about the Iraq war and U.S. soldiers being separated from their families, he will perseverate on this and question me as to why this is happening. In this sense, he is very concerned about politics to the extent that it impacts the lives of real people and families. During the first Iraq war, Kim was asked at a presentation what he thought about the war. He replied "Sadam shame" ('s a damn shame)!

Kim is most profoundly affected when tragedy begins to cast its shadow across the lives of innocent people, especially those who are vulnerable and can't help themselves, like seniors or children. He can get so disturbed that he literally makes himself physically ill.

One such incident transpired several years ago when, reading his morning paper as usual, Kim came across a story reporting a threat to Social Security for the elderly.

"What about the older people who need to have their Social Security checks to stay alive?" he asked me with alarm. "Are we going to let them starve?"

For two nights, every hour or so, he would sit on the edge of my bed and ask many of the same questions over and over again. No matter what I said to assure him things would work out, his mind would flash back to similar situations that had occurred in the past and his worry would only escalate.

Then, on Sunday morning, the last day of the fiscal government year, the news was broadcast that a temporary settlement on the national budget had been made by Congress. Kim's eyes brightened, his mouth stretched into a smile. "I knew it would happen like this," he said.

Then, he took my hand and said, "Dad, people who really care about people shouldn't frighten them with these kinds of scenarios. What can we do about our leaders who don't meet their responsibilities when they should?"

I put my other hand over his hand and said, "Maybe they need to talk with you?"

"When?" he asked.

Of all the scenarios that trouble Kim, what upsets him most is learning that harm has been done to children. Because he is entirely innocent and honest himself, Kim cannot comprehend how anyone could do anything as senseless as hurt a child. It does not make sense to him, and he will plead with me in vain for a logical explanation.

One day Kim was going through the morning paper, as he always does, covering each page in a matter of a few minutes. Suddenly, he came stomping into the kitchen, clearly distressed.

"What's the matter?" I asked. "What has upset you?"

He showed me the newspaper with the headline: "Missing Child's Body Located in Canal."

"Why was the baby wrapped up in its blanket and tied up with a rope?" he shouted uncontrollably. "So it wouldn't get wet? Why would the father bathe the baby with all those clothes on? Does all life begin in the water? I can't be wrapped in a blanket and cast adrift in a river. I'd catch cold!"

We walked into the living room and sat on the sofa. Suddenly, he leaped up, writhing in mental anguish, rubbing his hair profusely and then gripping his hands tightly, twisting them until they seemed they would come off his arms.

I pulled him back down onto the sofa and tried to comfort him. "It was a crazy thing, Kim," I tried to explain. "Whoever did it is sick in the head. Some people aren't able to cope with their problems and sometimes they do things that are bad, sometimes they don't even know they are doing them."

"Why, Dad? Why? That was just a tiny baby. He couldn't fight his father. You wouldn't hurt me like that, would you?"

"Of course not, " I said. "And maybe that father didn't mean to hurt his baby," I said.

"But he wrapped him in a blanket and tied him up so he couldn't get loose and then he put him in a canal. Why, Dad? Why can a father do something like that?"

It was a rough morning. Kim couldn't keep his breakfast down. He would be quiet and calm for a few minutes and then suddenly jump to his feet, leaping a foot or so into the air, and go through the same kind of questions.

It took over an hour to calm his fears.

"Want to take a short stroll and breathe in some of that pure air before we go to work?" I asked.

"A short walk might be good for us, Dad," he replied. We walked for a few minutes in silence before he said, "There are fathers who love their children all of the time, aren't there, Dad? And you are one of those, aren't you, Dad?"

He put his large, soft hand in mine, put his other arm around my neck and pulled my forehead to his. "Yes, Kim. I love you very much. No way could I ever harm you. You wouldn't hurt me either," I said.

He kissed me on the nose, real hard. By the time we got back home he was too tired to walk upstairs to his room. He just collapsed onto the sofa. I removed his shoes to the snoring sounds of peace at last.

Kim continues to be the very literal being he has always been, yet in recent years he has demonstrated that he can also make connections and form associations. As is the case for most savants, Kim's interests first manifest in rote memorization; however unlike most other savants, he has developed the capacity to comprehend much of the material he has committed to memory. He has also become a strikingly creative and versatile word mason within his chosen areas of expertise.

Sometimes his answers to questions or directions are quite concrete and literal. For instance, we were recently at a restaurant and, as is common, Kim was speaking too loudly. I told him, "Kim, lower your voice." His response was to slide lower down in his chair, almost underneath the table, thereby "lowering" his voice.

In other cases, his answers can seem quite ingenious. In one of his talks he answered the question, "Do you know Abraham Lincoln's Gettysburg Address?" by responding, "Will's house, 227 North West Front Street. But he stayed there only one night. He gave the speech the next day."

Kim intended no joke but when the audience laughed, he saw the humor in his response; since then, he has purposely recycled the story with humorous intent and effect.

Kim has learned that humor is an excellent way to engage an audience and make people happy. Over the past few years he has surprised me at presentations by blurting out numerous witty comments. It is sometimes difficult to tell whether he intended to make a joke or was simply speaking in his literal-minded way. Regardless, he has often made me and others burst out in laughter.

One such comment came when Kim and I were at a local college where Michael Moore of *Fareinheight 911* fame had just made an appearance. A news reporter asked Kim if he had gone to hear Moore's presentation. "No," said Kim. "Moore might be fair-in-height, but he is kind of obnoxious in so many other ways."

At a Pfizer medical dinner in New Jersey, a doctor in the audience asked Kim what he knew about President James Madison. Kim responded, "He had more problems with women than Bill Clinton did." The doctor then noted that there was an opportunity now for a woman to be nominated for Vice President (this was preceding the 2000 election), but it seemed she did not want to run. Kim responded: "You are talking about Elizabeth Dole, Secretary of Transportation. You guys here at Pfizer are responsible for her attitude. You put her husband, Bob Dole, on your Viagra commercials and now Elizabeth has no time to campaign."

Another time, during a question and answer session at a special awards dinner in Phoenix sponsored by the Good Will Industries of Arizona, Kim asked the president of the organization, who happened to be a Catholic priest, if he knew the Pope. The priest answered that he talked to the Pope in prayer every evening. Kim then remarked, in front of the entire room, that the church was having some problems getting men to join the priesthood and suggested that maybe the Pope should go to the Vatican crypt and talk with the monks who helped rewrite the bible about the typographical error in the King James version. The priest responded that he did not know what Kim was referring to. Kim's response shocked everyone in the room.

"They left the letter 'r' out of the word 'celebrate,'" he explained. "If they fix it, that might solve their problem."

At first a couple of people smiled, and then a wave of laughter engulfed the room. I looked at the priest and saw him cupping his hands over his face, trying to suppress a laugh.

At a gathering in Washington, D.C., where we were to deliver the annual disability training lecture to government officials, he quipped to the well-dressed and high-powered audience members, "Dad and I haven't seen so many ushers without flashlights in our whole life."

Dr. Treffert has been struck by Kim's undeniable power to make these kinds of clever connections and has written about his exceptional development. "The creative use of material that had originally been memorized by rote can be seen as the verbal equivalent of a musician's improvisation," Dr. Treffert explains. "Like the musician, Kim thinks quickly, so quickly that it can be difficult to keep up with his intricate associations. Often he seems two or three steps ahead of his audiences in his responses" (Christensen, D. & Treffert, D., 2005).

Within the past few years, Kim has also revealed what Dr. Treffert has called "a rather startling new dimension to his savant skills" (Christensen, D. & Treffert, D., 2005). This new dimension is in the realm of music. Although some savants exhibit exceptional musical talents and abilities, this phenomenon is usually confined to musical savants and is not common among prodigious memory savants such as Kim.

For many years Kim has revealed impressive abilities related to his love and recall of all kinds of music. He can name and sing almost any hit from the war years as well as tell you the name of the soloist and the band that recorded it. He delights in remembering and singing the hits of Elvis and the Beatles. He can also recall most of the music of the '70s, '80s and early '90s. But when he listens to opera or classical music, he disappears into a state of pure peacefulness. You can see and feel the excitement he is experiencing as his deep voice accentuates the chords and vibrates with the composer's music.

Much of Kim's love of classical music stems from his early childhood environment, listening to his mother play records on the phonograph. As they listened to the music together, he would read the albums' jacket covers. Today, he still remembers all the information from the jackets as well as the music. I believe he loves classical music almost as much as he loves people.

For many years Kim's recall of music and music history impressed us all, but only recently have we become aware of the full extent of his musical talents.

In 2002, Kim was introduced to Dr. April Greenan, director of the McKay Music Library and professor of music at the University of Utah. Although he had always enjoyed music, Kim did not appear to have any particular musical skills beyond factual recall of music history and styles. Because of Kim's difficulties with physical coordination, we assumed he would not be able to play an instrument.

Then, Kim once again did something that amazed us all. For several years, various production crews from other countries had filmed Kim interacting with Dr. Greenan. Generally, she would play excerpts from tapes or CDs and would occasionally play a piece of music on the piano. Kim would then identify the musical selections as well as the composer, when and where the composer was born and died, and when the particular piece was written.

One time, without any warning, she decided to try something new. "I know you think you are not physically coordinated to play the piano," she said softly, "but I want to try something. I want about five minutes to see if we can coordinate you on this grand piano. Will you let me try?"

Kim responded, "I can't play the piano. I can't read music. All I know is the music I heard when I was a little kid that my mom played on phonograph records while she studied her school work."

"And you remember almost every note on every record. Is that right?" asked Dr. Greenan.

"I think so," said Kim. "Okay, let's try it!"

Kim sat on the left side of the piano bench. Dr. Greenan sat on the right side. She began to press keys, one by one, and asked Kim if he could identify them. "F-major, C-flat, G-minor…"—he identified all 18 keys.

"You got every one right, Kim," exclaimed Dr. Greenan. "Let's continue. About 20 minutes ago, Kim, you hummed a composition written by J.S. Bach."

"It was Bach's Orchestral Suite No. 3," Kim replied.

"That's correct. But this time, I don't want you to sing it to me, I want you to play it on the piano. Will you do that?" asked Greenan.

"I haven't done this before. I am not physically coordinated. You know that," replied Kim. "But I will try to do it."

With his left hand (most savants are left handed), he slowly played each note.

"Kim," smiled Dr. Greenan, "you got every note exactly right!"

Kim looked at her and remarked, "But Bach played it like this!" He played the notes very quickly, at the pace Bach played them. Then, he reached his right hand over the top of his left hand as he continued to play the original keys and added chords to the exercise.

"Why are you playing the chord sounds over the music theme?" asked Greenan.

"That's how you professional piano players cover up the mistakes you might make on your main hand," Kim concluded.

They sat together at the piano as Dr. Greenan identified compositions from Mozart, Wagner, Bach, Brahms, Mahler, Bruckner, and several operatic selections. Kim played parts of each composition.

"What are you playing now?" asked Greenan.

"I just played the clarinet's part for you. Now, I will play the trumpets, next come the violins, the violas," Kim explained. "Isn't that the way you hear the music?"

Dr. Greenan looked over to me and said, "How does he know the parts each instrument must play?"

I, too, was mystified. He had never talked to me about instruments, although at a concert several years ago in St. Louis he did give a clue of this talent. We were invited backstage to meet with a conductor and several of the board members of the symphony and Kim asked the conductor why he had had selected Bruckner that night when Mahler was seven minutes shorter and much more interesting. The conductor politely replied, "We have been practicing Bruckner for some 10 months and felt it was a good piece for our orchestra."

"And when did your second trombone join your orchestra?" asked Kim. Puzzled, the conductor responded, "About two months ago, why?"

"You know he came in two notes late in the third segment," replied Kim.

"I can't believe this," the conductor responded. "Last Friday night he did the same thing!"

Dr. Treffert has marveled at Kim's musical talent:

> He possesses complete knowledge of the instruments in the traditional symphony orchestra and readily identifies the timbre of any instrumental passage. For example, he

> presented the opening of Bedrich Smetana's orchestral tone poem, The Moldau, by reducing the flute and clarinet parts to an arpeggiated figure in his left hand and explaining that the oboes and bassoons enter with the primary theme, which he then reduced to pitches played singly and then in thirds by his right hand (the left-hand figure continuing as it does in the score). His comprehension of musical styles is demonstrated in his ability to identify composers of pieces he had not previously heard by assessing the piece's musical style and deducing who that composer might be.
> (Christensen, D. & Treffert, D., 2005)

Currently, many of the groups we interact with ask Kim if he will play the piano at their meetings. He never does. He will only play the piano when Dr. Greenan is at his side. "She is the person who makes me coordinated," smiles Kim.

Dr. Greenan continues to meet with us whenever a film crew comes to town to meet Kim. She is also doing some in-depth studying with him, hoping that he will learn how to compose music. "I hope we can somehow capture the genius that seems to be locked inside his feelings and knowledge about music," she says.

Within a short period of working with Dr. Greenan, Kim learned to play the piano and was able to enhance his discussion of compositions by playing passages from them, demonstrating on the keyboard many of the pieces he recalled from his massive mental library. Kim also has remarkable long-term memory of pitch, remembering the original pitch level of each composition.

Though Kim is still physically awkward, his manual dexterity is improving. When seated at the piano with Dr. Greenan, he may play the piece he wishes to discuss and sing the passage of interest or describe the music verbally, shifting seamlessly from one mode to another. Kim pays attention to rhythm as well, lightly tapping the beat on his chest with his right hand or, when playing the piano, tapping his right foot.

Greenan, a Mozart scholar, made the following observations:

> Kim's knowledge of music is considerable. His ability to recall every detail of a composition he has heard—in many cases only once and more than 40 years ago—is astonishing. The connections he draws between and weaves through compositions, composer's lives, historical events, movie sound tracks and thousands of facts stored in his database reveal enormous intellectual capacity. (Christensen, D. & Treffert, D., 2005)

She even compares Kim to Mozart, who also had an enlarged head, a fascination with numbers and uneven social skills.

For 52 years, everyone, including Kim and me, thought that he was not physically capable of activities that required motor coordination. Doctors have speculated that, in addition to causing him to lose the ability to reason, the damage to his cerebellum as a young child may have deterred him from developing full physical coordination. It is clear that this damage affected his head and eye movements, and is possibly the cause of his frequent speech eruptions and repetitive statements.

However, in light of his newfound ability to play the piano, I have come to wonder whether perhaps being told he was not coordinated led Kim to develop a psychological belief that prevented him from learning some of the fundamentals of caring for himself. Might it be that some of his "inabilities" to fend for himself were caused by us not trying to teach these skills to him as a child? Did we promote a kind of learned helplessness in him? Maybe he has learned to manipulate his special needs for assistance so that he can spend more time reading and learning?

I also cannot help but wonder about future discoveries of even more talents Kim may possess. I particularly wonder about his potential to use computers, as that would surely open up a whole new world of knowledge and information to him. To date, he has been very resistant to using computers and has actually stonewalled attempts to get him involved.

During the summer of 2006, a young woman who was working on a video visited us in Salt Lake City. At that time, she tried to work with Kim to explore the computer keyboard. At first, he became agitated. "I can't do this," he claimed. "There are billions of sites but sometimes it is too risky to use them." When she suggested that he might like to read the newspaper online, he said he wouldn't like that and wouldn't be able to follow it. "I like to be around the newspaper," he explained.

With reluctance Kim sits at the computer

Although we have tried to convince Kim of the great potential that his being able to use the computer holds, he remains reticent to try. It seems he associates the use of computers with something frightening. This may be because at around the same time we tried introducing him to the computer his siblings and I talked with him about plans for the future, when I am no longer able to care for him. Perhaps he associates the use of the computer with me not being around. When I am using my computer at home he does not like to come into the room.

I remain hopeful that, in the future, Kim may overcome his aversion to computers. Although I am not an expert on computers by any means, I have read and have been told that that there are a wide array of assistive technology programs available for people with disabilities. Perhaps we will identify a device or program that will make Kim more comfortable and willing to explore computers.

CHAPTER 9
Sharing the Same Shadow: Challenges of Parenting a Special Needs Child

Looking back on my life with Kim brings me great joy and great pride. He has grown and matured in ways I could never have imagined. People so often focus on his unique abilities to recall even the smallest of facts, and indeed he has enormous mental capacity. But in my interactions with him I am so frequently reminded that the only part of him that is larger than his brain is his heart. I love him completely.

It has been a long, exciting, often frustrating, wonderful journey, and I feel truly blessed. Kim has made me feel more strongly about how valuable life is. We've struggled at times, but at the end of the day I feel that our struggles have made us stronger, brought us closer, and allowed us to help others see different parts of life and meet different kinds of people. Kim has turned my life around 180 degrees. He's a very literal person, but also has a unique brand of intellectual curiosity that causes him to think about some incredible things. He makes me ask a lot of questions I would never otherwise have asked.

Recently, Kim has been talking to me about quantum mechanics. He tells me he wants to get quantum mechanics into our lives so that we can go to the fifth or sixth dimension to get away from the limited mentality of the present human race. He has also told NASA to hurry along their work to get us nearer to these new dimensions. I don't exactly understand what he's talking about—I guess my brain is stuck in the limited mentality of the present human race—but I'm sure he's on to something!

Several years ago, a psychiatrist asked Kim about our "unique symbiotic relationship." Kim's response rendered me speechless: "Dad and I share the same shadow." When I heard this, my heart beat double time. Doctors say he can't reason; I think his statement came from his heart, not from his brain.

People who know us well and even most people who just meet us briefly have commented on our unusually interconnected relationship. *Rain Man* screenwriter Barry Morrow told an interviewer for a recent documentary on Kim,

> When I think about Kim's future, I can't help but think about what we lose when we lose Fran. What we lose is the interpreter. Fran is the code talker because Kim speaks in elliptical ways and Fran knows all the pieces of the puzzle that Kim isn't sharing because he's past it already. Fran walks behind like the elephant, sweeping up, while Kim marches on forward

> with all this going on, and if we don't have Fran there who's going to tell us what we're missing? (Hofer, P. & Rockenhaus, F., 2006)

Barry's words really captured the essence of our relationship. Not only are we emotionally close, but we have developed our own way of communicating and understanding one another. Even though Kim knows the answer to just about any question you can throw at him, he doesn't always reply in a clear, understandable way. He often speaks entirely in predicates, leaving the subjects quietly resting in his thoughts. I try to get him to tell me the subjects so that we can complete the circle. Once he does so, his comments become clear and meaningful.

Over the years, I have become able to follow Kim's erratic trains of thought. He tends to fixate on the memories of certain experiences we have had or information he's read that has been particularly noteworthy to him, either because he found it amusing or it was a highly covered news story. Any number of statements or questions can trigger an association with these memories.

Once the association has been made, Kim is off. Without offering a clue or making any segue, he will begin to quote a person or a headline, or sing a song that he relates to whatever he has just heard. Because he frequently returns to the same memories, I can often decipher what he's making reference to and how he made that connection. I used to have to ask him to explain some of his erratic topic shifts, but now, before I can even ask, he will volunteer, "You know how I got that, Dad?" Usually I do, and when I don't he explains it to me in a way that probably no one but I could understand.

Through spending so much time with Kim and through his talking to me about much of what he learns, I am perhaps one of the world's most knowledgeable non-savants! Occasionally, I find his incessant questions and explanations of news items and other subjects a bit frustrating, but usually patience prevails.

When Kim's talking—which is most of the time—it's almost impossible for me to concentrate on activities that require focus. He speaks very loudly and quickly, and gets very animated when he talks about things that interest him, making it difficult for me to concentrate on anything or be productive. The only time I can reliably expect to be able to read, write checks, prepare correspondence or make phone calls without interruption is when Kim is asleep, so I often end up having to do most of these tasks between midnight and 2:00 a.m., at which time he's snoring like a locomotive.

Sometimes I wonder just how Kim truly feels about our relationship. He does not usually talk about his feelings and has difficulty verbalizing emotions, yet every once in a while he will say something that hits upon the true nature of his feelings about the pair of us. Of course the most poignant comment was probably his reference to us sharing the same shadow, but another, more recent example also stands out in my mind.

It had snowed a great deal on one particular night, with over six inches covering our patio. Kim worries about the weather… *really* worries about it! Being preoccupied with the snow, he had been walking up and down the stairs, obsessively checking on the status of the weather and monitoring accumulation totals throughout the night. Just as it was time to get up, Kim came into my bedroom, sat down on my arm, cupped his large hands around my face, peered into my eyes from about six inches away and whispered, "Dad, being with you is so important to me. You are the father of my heart." I don't know what made him say that, but I know that the words came from the bottom of his heart.

As most parents of children with disabilities will tell you: "We have a 30/10 schedule—30 hours every day and 10 days per week." It is so true! Having a child with a disability means sometimes short changing others—and oneself . The special needs of the child must come first, which can be difficult for others to understand and accept. Sometimes people become resentful, even angry. Creating this balance between the challenges of a child with disabilities and the needs of other family members is indeed monumental. It isn't always possible for a parent to be successful on both counts. Perhaps this is where the phrase, "fair is not always equal" needs to be considered.

Over the years I have become more sensitive to this and try not to give other people short shrift, but try as I may, there is a reality to our circumstances that other people need to understand, and which I try to explain. I hope that others will try to understand the difficult position of the caregiver. If people could walk around in the shoes of parents of children with disabilities for a while, I am sure they'd be a lot more patient!

I have discovered that having a routine makes our lives much easier and I encourage other parents to try to implement routines. Fortunately, Kim is a big fan of routines, as are most autistic individuals. When we're not traveling, our days look pretty much the same. We get up early, before 5:30 a.m. I have to help Kim use the electric razor, shower, and then we select the clothes he will wear for the day.

While he is getting dressed I go downstairs to prepare breakfast. Often at the breakfast table I will notice that he's put his shirt on backwards or has put his shoes on the wrong feet. I believe this is due to his preoccupation with a constant stream of thoughts that distracts him from focusing on dressing himself.

The first thing Kim does when he comes downstairs in the morning is read the newspaper. He asks me dozens of questions about items in the paper as he reads, and I have to remind him that I haven't had a chance to read the paper myself yet!

When breakfast is ready, he immediately goes to the dining room table and begins to eat. He eats very quickly and has usually gotten his dishes to the kitchen sink by the time I sit down at the table. After breakfast, I help him finish getting dressed and comb his hair. Once he is dressed and ready he locates the journal that he will take with him to the library in the afternoon. He is constantly working in his journal, though I am never sure what exactly he is working on. This is one area in which he demands some privacy and I am happy to give it to him, though I am intrigued and will occasionally ask him about his project. Sometimes he will explain, other times he will not.

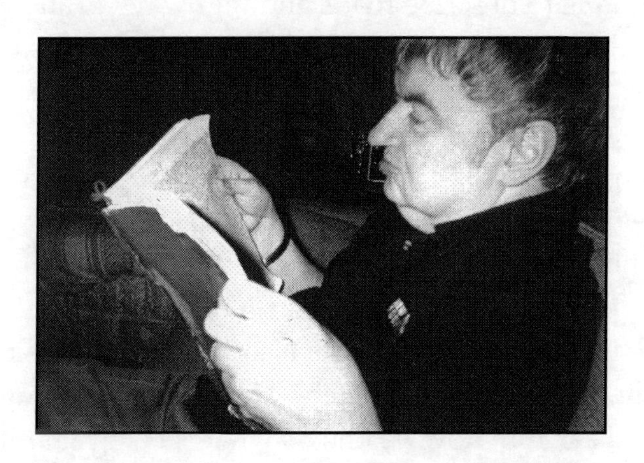

One project that Kim has told me about is entering data about people with similar surnames who live in cities in Europe and in the United States that have approximately the same populations and the same last four digits of their telephone numbers. Sometimes, if population figures are difficult to match, he uses the area measurements of similarly populated cities to connect the two.

It's a very complicated process. I haven't been able to comprehend all of the details, and I certainly don't understand where he gets the idea for such projects. Only Kim seems to understand the exact process. I have cautiously watched and tried to figure out what he is doing as he works on his journal, but I really can only speculate with wonder. Ultimately, I don't know the significance of his journal projects, except that they incorporate a lot of names, numbers and places.

As part of his journal projects matching names and places, Kim has studied hundreds of telephone directories of American cities. He also studies atlases and is able to describe roads and highways to and from almost every town or city in the U.S., the area codes, zip codes, counties, historical events that have occurred in or near the city, and the television stations—by channel number and call letters—that can be seen in that particular city. He also knows the telephone companies that serve each city.

At home, Kim spends most of his time reading. Sometimes while he reads he also watches television. Oddly, when he does "watch" TV, he sets it on mute. When I ask him how he knows what is being said if he doesn't have the sound on he tells me he can hear what's going on. I assume he can. Sometimes he will laugh with the people on the tube. I hear nothing.

Often he reads two or three books at the same time, quickly going back and forth between selections. Whether they are angled on his bed or upside down, he seems to be able to read each of them for a few minutes before looking at the next one. He also memorizes each week's TV Guide and knows all the programs' schedules.

When we visit someone in their home, the first thing Kim does is seek out their book collection. He then spends time leafing through the books that interest him for a few minutes each. He enjoys finding copies of books in other peoples' homes that we also have in our home library.

While reading, he occasionally continues to twist a piece of cord in front of his face, while making droning noises which seem to allow him to fully focus on the information at hand.

Kim is generally easygoing and happy to cooperate, but like anyone else, he has his moments! Sometimes we get to a presentation and he doesn't feel like talking, or he doesn't want to talk about a particular subject. At such times, I have to repeatedly give him instructions and ask him to cooperate; sometimes he listens to me, and sometimes he doesn't! Usually this stubbornness doesn't last long, though, and if we are presenting he most often comes around within a few minutes and rejoins the group.

Yes, Kim and I share the same shadow, and I can't imagine my life without him. Frighteningly, I was faced with that prospect a few years ago when Kim took ill.

It was just before Christmas, 2000. The ground was dressed in white and dozens of lengthy icicles hung outside Kim's bedroom window. Christmas lights dotted the greens outside our condominium, but Kim didn't seem very interested in the outside world. He seemed a bit listless. He rested on the sofa in the living room much of the day. He didn't have any interest in going to the library to work on his journal.

He had put on a few noticeable pounds of softness and was experiencing some shortness of breath. His face appeared swollen, but he didn't complain about not feeling well. His appetite was good. The droning noises he usually makes when reading weren't as frequent or pronounced.

I came to suspect something was not right, so I called the doctor and expressed my concern. "Bring him in tomorrow morning," the doctor told me.

The next day, the doctor examined him and told me that he was filling with fluids and that his heart was having some minor aberrations. Also, his lungs were tight. He suggested I take him to a cardiologist right away. That afternoon, I called the cardiologist and explained the situation. He asked me if I could bring Kim in to see him the next morning.

The examination took a couple of hours. The machine Kim was made to lay in reminded him of his experiences in MRI machines. "Except, Dad, there wasn't that loud droning noise the MRI shared with me," Kim said.

When the results came back the doctor talked to me about his thoughts and observations. He was concerned but was optimistic that Kim would respond to drug therapy. He gave me several prescriptions and said to bring Kim back to the office in two weeks.

Over the next few weeks, Kim's neck and cheeks remained puffy and bloated, but his routine activities—reading and pacing and talking—seemed quite normal. He made visits to a couple of schools and a church, but he didn't want to walk among the audience as he usually did. Instead, he chose to just sit on a chair in front of the groups and field questions. He seemed to tire more quickly and easily, yet he refused to stop being active.

After two weeks, Kim and I returned to the cardiologist to find out how he was doing on the medications. Kim didn't seem concerned about the severity of the situation, but he understood that there was a problem and, as usual, he asked me lots of questions. He talked about his uncle's death from a mitral valve malfunction and asked (with curiosity but no fear) whether that was what was wrong with him. I assured him it was not.

Over the years Kim has had some bad experiences with doctors (he frequently references the time in his childhood when we took him to a doctor who abruptly told us to institutionalize him before rushing off to a golf game) and doesn't always trust them. Fortunately, he assured me that he liked this doctor and would listen to him because the doctor's father had also been a cardiologist. He was further impressed that the doctor's picture and awards were displayed in the hospital's hallway.

As we waited in the reception room for the doctor to give his diagnosis, Kim didn't seem nervous. He talked to an elderly couple, asking them where they had lived besides Salt Lake City. The man had grown up in a small town in Minnesota. Kim told him the roads to his town, its area code, zip code, the county, the television stations in his town, the telephone company that serviced the area, and the year, date, and day of the week that Minnesota became a state. He told the man's wife, who was 73, the day she was born and the day she would become 74. The secretary asked if he could tell her about her birthday. In a few seconds he told her the day she was born, the day her birthday would fall on in the current year, and the year and day of the week she would turn 65 so she could retire. "How do you do that?" she asked. "I know my savantism," Kim replied.

Finally, the doctor was ready to see Kim. He walked over, shook Kim's hand and greeted him warmly. "How are things going? How do you feel, Kim?" the doctor asked. Kim stood up, took my left arm, and said to the doctor, "It's time to know what you want to do with me. Let's go into your exam room." He was ready to get down to business.

At first, Kim was hesitant to remove his shirt, telling the doctor that he normally had his blood pressure taken from inside his arm. "We will take your blood pressure in a minute, but first I want to listen to your heart and lungs," the doctor said. The door opened and a nurse wheeled in a machine with lots of wires on it.

"An encephalogram machine?" asked Kim. "Is my brain in control of my heart?"

"No," replied the doctor, "we just want to put some receptors on your chest area and measure how everything is going on inside you." The doctor removed the stethoscope from his neck, took Kim's pulse, and felt around his neck and arms. "I will be back in about five minutes, Kim, as soon as the nurse finishes the test."

"I hope she studied for it," Kim responded.

About 10 minutes passed before the doctor returned. He said to me, "It's pretty serious. He is in the early stages of congestive heart failure. We are making hospital admittance arrangements right now. In a few minutes, we will escort you over to the hospital to the ICU ward. He is packing a lot of water and other fluids in his body and it's pressing into his heart and lungs. We will be able to get him treated quickly in the ICU and should be able to get everything back to normal."

Kim listened to everything that was said. Then he looked at me and said, "Dad, it's time to get me back to my regular self. Let's go over to the ICU. Will you stay with me if I have to be there over night?"

The doctor smiled and said, "Kim, your dad will be with you all the time. We'll put a lounging chair right in the room beside you. You'll be able to talk to him day and night for a couple of days. Is that OK with you?"

"It's important for me to be with dad when he worries about what I'm going to do next. Dad, did you bring your pajamas?" Kim asked.

The five days Kim spent in the ICU felt endless. In the evenings, his mom and her husband came by. His brother and sister and Mary Ruth with the Gold Tooth also visited. Many friends left "get well soon" messages on our home telephone answering machine and sent Kim cards.

Kim was a perfect patient. He chatted with nurses, doctors and technicians during the night as well as the day. One night nurse was surprised when Kim told her she was three minutes late. "You should have been here at 3:20 a.m., but its 3:23," he told her. "How did he know the time, there's no clock in the room?" Kim lifted his watch to his face and pushed the light-button. "Don't you remember, Dad, when you gave me this new watch for Christmas? The battery still works."

Fortunately, Kim made excellent progress once his treatment got underway. After five days he was moved to a double room on another floor and I was invited to share the other bed with him for two more days. Within a few days he shed massive amounts of fluid and was allowed to come home. I monitored him closely and was relieved to note that his condition continued to improve.

A few days later, we returned to the doctor who greeted Kim with a warm hug. He led us into the exam room where three doctors were waiting. Several X-rays were displayed on the wall.

"No damage, anywhere," said the doctor. "Kim will need to rest for awhile. If things go as I'm sure they will, he should be back to his regular activities in a couple of weeks."

I was incredibly relieved to hear that Kim's heart functioning had gone from 25 percent of normal at the time of admission to 80 percent when he was discharged. Today, it's up to 98 percent.

"We at the hospital have one request, Kim" concluded the doctor. "Will you bring your dad over to see us about once a week for the next month? There are a few people here who didn't get to find out when they will retire."

Since then, we have continued to return to the doctor's office every three months for a checkup. Now and then, we walk over to the cardiovascular department in the hospital and say "hi" to some very special friends.

I am eternally grateful to the wonderful doctors who cared for and continue to care for Kim. I think this close call was far scarier for me that it was for him.

I faced a close call of my own several years back, also with my heart. In August of 2001, I had two "silent" heart attacks. Rather than have major heart surgery to repair the problem, I chose to have my heart "patched up." Because of Kim's needs, I didn't feel I could be out of commission for an extended period of time. Much like any parent would do, I chose to put my child's needs before my own. Fortunately, the heart stents have been effective so far, and doctors are pleased with my overall health as well as Kim's.

While filming the DVD *Celebrating Diversity*, (2007) I had the privilege of meeting a young woman who interviewed Kim and myself and spent time with us in Salt Lake City. I was deeply touched by a letter she sent to me shortly after her visit. In it, she beautifully expressed the essence of my relationship with my son.

Kim and Angela Hanson Garofalo, 2006

Dear Fran,

It was wonderful to spend time with you and Kim last week, and I am so excited about the production we are working on together. It will most certainly be a terrific opportunity for students and the greater community to learn more about Kim's message. In a way the title says it all, *Celebrating Diversity.*

Because I spent time alone with Kim in his own community, I became even more aware of his special qualities. But, Fran, that also gave me new insight into your unbelievable role with Kim. He is a delight, but being with him requires enormous patience and dedication. Yes, Kim's "savantness" is amazing. But equally amazing is your ability to support and maintain this gift.

So much of Kim would be lost if it were not for your ability to connect, interpret and frame his comments and conversation. His verbal wanderings would be just that, wanderings, if you were not able to relate them to experiences and history, and the observer would be lost. I particularly liked hearing you described as Kim's "sequetarian." Many of his comments would be meaningless to the listener if you did not put them into perspective. And I realized for the first time how much mental and emotional energy this takes; you must always be 100 percent alert. I was amazed at how even if you are talking with someone else you seem to always have an eye and ear on Kim, ready to support and assist .

But Fran, as important as that all is, the sameness of your shadow goes so beyond the

> mere physical and conversational; the very essence of who you are is what Kim shares so vividly. You are a consummate model for Kim, not just in what you say but what you do. When Kim presents his message it is certainly one he believes in, but primarily because he sees it "in action" in your life. He is a reflection of who you are. His value system comes from you, Fran, and his focus on respecting, accepting, rejoicing and celebrating are an embodiment of you. How fortunate your son is to always know he has your unconditional love. (Angela Hanson Garafolo, National Professional Resources, Inc., personal communication)

That letter brought a lump to my throat, and a tear to my eye.

Yes, I think frequently about how close Kim and I are to one another. I am grateful beyond words to be sharing a shadow with someone so special. But I am also exceedingly aware of the issues this presents for the future.

CHAPTER 10
Tomorrow, Tomorrow, Tomorrow...

More and more over the past few years, people ask me the question, "What are your plans for Kim should something happen to you?" Good question. This concern has bombarded my mind for many years and weighs daily on my thoughts.

The future is a concern for every parent, but especially for parents of children with disabilities. I am in my eighties and although I'm in relatively good health, I can definitely feel the effects of aging. I have less energy and move more slowly, which at times troubles me because there are still so many things I want to do in life.

Sometimes, when Kim and I board an airplane, I find myself thinking, "Maybe the airplane will crash. That would be the perfect answer. We'd both go at once, together." But that's a terrible way to look at things. I would hate for the world to lose Kim and his special mind. I'm old and have had a full, rich life, so it wouldn't be such a tragedy for this fate to befall me. But it would be a tremendous tragedy for those who know and love Kim, as well as those who have not yet had the chance to meet him, to lose him before his time.

Realistically, I will probably pass before Kim, so I have been careful to make detailed arrangements for his future once I am gone. The issue of providing for Kim financially has long been complicated. He is only insurable through Medicaid, which is a blessing and a curse. Medicaid requires that he only have assets up to $2,000. Any more than that and he loses his coverage. He's already lost it once.

In honor of his contribution to the movie *Rain Man*, Dustin Hoffman initiated a trust fund for Kim. Being unexpectedly presented with a $10,000 trust fund was an incredible honor, and we will forever be grateful for Dustin's thoughtfulness. No one anticipated this gift would present a problem, since the trust was not touchable until I was gone. But Medicaid said that since it had Kim's name on it, the $10,000 trust was an asset, thus disqualifying him for Medicaid. We ended up having to spend half the money to pay legal fees, and ultimately my only option was to transfer the rest of the money to his brother and sister so that Kim didn't lose his coverage.

Kim's brother and sister will be the executors of my estate and will have joint power of attorney to make decisions for Kim's welfare. Because of the restrictions on assets for Kim, all of my assets (home, bank accounts, stocks) are in my name only and will belong to my two younger children as recipients of my will.

Throughout his life Kim has had to rely on disability benefits from Social Security as his sole source of income. We apportion this income to cover a quarter of our basic living expenses. The money just barely covers that. I had not accepted fees when Kim spoke to groups until recently, when it became financially necessary to do so. I am not interested in profiting from our engagements; my only concern is to be able to provide for our needs. For years I asked organizations that have the resources to make donations to programs in their areas that serve children with special needs. I still encourage this whenever possible.

My recommendations to parents of children with disabilities: Try to keep your children on Medicaid while you're alive. Make plans for after you're gone, and make sure to have your estate signed over to someone who will take care of your child. Have extensive discussions with this person to make sure that he or she is clear on your wishes for your child's future care and will be able to carry them out.

I don't think anyone else could single-handedly take care of Kim the way I do, but the reality is he will continue to need round-the-clock care. We have visited several senior care facilities in Utah and in nearby states, interacting with the residents and staff and looking over their operations. I have found many independent living centers and full-care senior retirement facilities that provide the 24-hour care and special assistance Kim requires.

One of the primary criteria for me in assessing a facility for Kim is that the patients must have the opportunity for significant social interaction and have access to stimulating activities. Kim needs intellectual companionship as well as physical assistance with showering, dressing, oral hygiene, food preparation, getting to medical appointments, acquiring reading materials, etc. It is essential that books, newspapers and magazines be available to Kim and that staff has the time and interest to listen to him, even when his conversation seems disjointed. It is very important to me that people who take care of Kim take the time to get to know him, understand his needs, and appreciate his gifts.

When we were visiting a senior facility recently I asked Kim what he thought about living in such a place. His response was typically simplistic: "It would be good, Dad, if they would fix my breakfast and lunch and dinner, and help me in the shower. And I could talk with lots of people." And then he veered off to another topic. I tried to bring him back to the topic by mentioning that he may have to be more independent, but I was unable to get any further feedback from him. However, perhaps by coincidence or perhaps by design, the next day Kim organized many of the magazines in our house and said, "I am just trying to help you more, Dad!"

The topic of death is not one we have delved into at length, but Kim appears to take the passing of people rather unemotionally. He makes comments such as, "he or she will be happier now." I don't usually take him to wakes or funerals as he tends to become the center of attention and I don't think that's appropriate. However when he asked to go to the wake of a friend of his from the workshop he had worked at, I had no reservations about taking him along.

At the funeral home, the deceased man's mother asked Kim how he thought her son looked. Very seriously, Kim replied: "He looks just like he looked every day at work...sound asleep!" His mother laughed and once again I was reminded of Kim's total innocence and literalness.

I have bought a funeral plot that is two deep so that Kim and I can be together even after we're gone. I've made sure to keep detailed records of everything about Kim, from his medical history to his daily routine, so that there are no unanswered questions about how to care for him when I'm gone.

I would be lying if I said I didn't worry about the future, but at the end of the day I can rest assured that I have done all of the necessary planning for the next phase of Kim's life. When Barry Morrow was interviewed for a recent documentary on Kim, he commented on his thoughts about Kim's future:

> He's not going to slip away and be lost to some backward institution. It isn't going to happen. Not when television stations all over the world and magazines and movies have made him into a world icon, and he is the most unusual person to perhaps ever live. (Hofer, P. & Rickenhaus, F., 2006)

As a parent I have sometimes questioned whether I have made the right choices for Kim, but considering how it has all turned out and how far he has exceeded what others expected of him when he was initially diagnosed as mentally retarded as an infant, I have no regrets.

Due to the continuing interest in savants and brain research, Kim has been the subject of a number of documentaries and television programs as well as hundreds of newspaper and magazine articles. Among them: ABC's *20/20* and *Good Morning, America*; Family Network's *Unbelievable*; TBS' *Ripley's Believe it or Not!*; NBC's *Today Show;* Vancouver, BC's *Today Show*; Focus Productions' *The Real Rain Man* (shown in the U.S. on The Discovery Channel); the Scientific America articles *Island of Genius* (2002) and *Inside the Mind of a Savant*

(2004); Salt Lake City's *Braniac*; and television productions in Germany, Poland, England, Sweden, Australia, Tokyo and more.

His life today is filled with studies of his brain by neurologists, psychologists, psychiatrists, scientists and researchers who are conducting studies on everything from genetics and DNA to dementia and Alzheimers disease. In addition to potentially providing meaningful contributions to science, learning about and coming to understand savants and Savant Syndrome can provide insight to our potential as human beings. As stated by Dr. Treffert:

> We can learn that the handicap need not necessarily blur hope and that stereotyping and labeling serve only to obscure, in a pernicious manner, an individual's strengths. We can learn the difference between paucity of emotion and purity of emotion. From the families, teachers and therapists of the savant we can learn that, in dealing with people who have problems, sometimes severe ones, it is not enough to care for those people, we must care about them as well. We can learn that there is a difference between sharing the spirit and shaping the spirit. We can learn how to work with a differently shaped soul—to understand, to actualize and to appreciate it—while still respecting its uniqueness (Treffert, D., 2006, p. 318).

REFERENCES

Christensen, D. & Treffert, D. (2005, December). Inside the mind of a savant. *Scientific American*.

Collins, L. (2004, November 7). NASA scientists taking a peek at Utahn's brain. *Desert Morning News*.

Feltes, S. (Producer, Director). (2006).*The real rain man* [DVD]. Bristol, UK: Focus Productions.

Hanson, R. (Producer). (2007). *Celebrating diversity: A universal message from the real rain man* [DVD]. Port Chester, NY: National Professional Resources, Inc.

Höfer, P. & Röckenhaus, F. (Producers, Writers, Directors). (2006). *Beautiful minds- A voyage into the brain. Episode 1: The memory masters* [DVD]. Dortmund, Germany: colourFIELD tell-a-vision.

McKie, R. (2005, December 11). NASA ties to figure out real-life Rain Man's brain. *The Observer*.

Nilsson, A. (Producer). (2006). *Mot Kim Peek: Verklighetens Rainman* [Television documentary]. Stockholm, Sweden: TV4 AB.

Peek, Fran. (1996). *The real Rain Man*. Salt Lake City, UT: Harkness Publishing Consultants. (Rights now held by National Professional Resources, Inc., Port Chester, NY)

Treffert, D. Is there a little Rain Man in each of us? Retrieved March 3, 2007, from http://www.wisconsinmedicalsociety.org/savant/eachus.cfm.

Treffert, D. (2006 edition). *Extraordinary people: Understanding savant syndrome*. Lincoln, NE: iUniverse, Inc.

Treffert, D. & Wallace, G. (2002, June). Islands of genius: Artistic brilliance and a dazzling memory can sometimes accompany autism and other developmental disorders. *Scientific American*.

Appendix A

RESOURCES: Savant

Web Sites

Dr. Darold Treffert's Website
http://www.daroldtreffert.com/

Wisconsin Medical Society Resource List
http://www.wisconsinmedicalsociety.org/savant/resourcelist.cfm

Savant Syndrome
http://www.healthofchildren.com/S/Savant-Syndrome.html

Savants: Charting 'Islands of Genius'
http://www.cnn.com/2006/HEALTH/09/06/savant.genius/index.html

The Rain Man's Disorder: Savant Syndrome
http://rarediseases.about.com/cs/neurodisorders/a/052502.htm

Centre for the Mind
http://www.centreforthemind.com/

Savant Syndrome
http://www.neurodiversity.com/savant.html

Print and Media

Beautiful Minds: A Voyage Into the Brain
A documentary produced by Colourfied Productions of Dortmund, Germany

The Real Rain Man
A documentary produced by Focus Productions, Bristol England, in the United States, aired on The Discovery Channel in U.S.

Brainman
A documentary produced by Focus Productions, Bristol England, in the United States, aired on The Discovery Channel in U.S.

Extraordinary People: Understanding Savant Syndrome, 2006

Treffert, Darold, & D. Christensen. "Inside the Mind of a Savant," *Scientific American*, June/July 2006, pg. 108-113.

Treffert, Darold, & G. Wallace. "Islands of Genius," *Scientific American*, June 2002, Volume 286, No. 6, pg. 76-85.

Peek, Fran (1996). *The Real Rain Man.* Harkness Publishing Consultants, Salt Lake City, Utah.

Appendix B

RESOURCES: Disabilities

Organizations

American Association on Mental Retardation
444 North Capitol Street, NW
Suite 846
Washington, D.C. 20001-1512
(800) 424-3688
www.aaidd.org

American Speech-Language-Hearing Association (ASHA)
10801 Rockville Pike
Rockville, Maryland 20852
(800) 638-8255
www.asha.org

The Arc of the United States
1010 Wayne Avenue, Suite 650
Silver Spring, MD 20910
(301) 565-3842
www.thearc.org

Autism Society of America
7910 Woodmont Avenue, Suite 300
Bethesda, Maryland 20814-3067
(800) 328-8476
www.autism-society.org

Council for Exceptional Children (CEC)
1110 North Glebe Road, Suite 300
Arlington, VA 22201-5704
(800) 224-6830
www.cec.sped.org

Exceptional Parent
700-76 Broadway #360
Westwood, NJ 07675
(877) 372-7368
www.eparent.com

Institute on Community Integration
University of Minnesota
102 Pattee Hall, 150 Pillsbury Drive SE
Minneapolis MN 55455
(612) 624-6300
http://ici.umn.edu

Learning Disabilities Association of America (LDA)
Sheila Buckley - Executive Director
4156 Library Road
Pittsburgh, PA 15234-1349
(412) 341-1515
www.ldaamerica.org

Special Olympics
1133 19th Street, N.W.
Washington, DC 20036 USA
(202) 628-3630
www.specialolympics.org

National Center for Learning Disabilities
381 Park Avenue South Suite 1401
New York, NY 10016
(888) 575-7373
www.ncld.org

National Down Syndrome Congress
1370 Center Drive, Suite 102
Atlanta, GA 30338
(800) 232.NDSC
www.ndsccenter.org

National Federation of the Blind
1800 Johnson Street
Baltimore, MD 21230
(410) 659-9314
www.nfb.org

National Information Center for Children
and Youth with Disabilities
P.O. Box 1492
Washington, DC 20013
(800) 695-0285
www.nichcy.org

National Organization on Disability (NOD)
910 Sixteenth Street, N.W.
Suite 600
Washington, DC 20006
(202) 293-5960
www.nod.org

Office of Special Education Programs (OSEP)
U.S. Department of Education
400 Maryland Ave., S.W.
Washington, DC 20202-7100
http://www.ed.gov/about/offices/list/osers/osep/

Office of Special Education and Rehabilitative Services
U.S. Department of Education, (OSERS)
400 Maryland Ave., S.W.
Washington, DC 20202-7100
http://www.ed.gov/about/offices/list/osers/

TASH, 1025 Vermont Ave., Floor 7
Washington, DC 20005
(202) 263-5600
www.tash.org

United Cerebral Palsy Association
1660 L Street, NW, Suite 700, Washington, DC 20036
(800) 872-5827
www.ucp.org

United Way of America
701 N. Fairfax Street
Alexandria, VA 22314
www.unitedway.org

World Ability Federation
120 S. Riverside Plaza
Chicago, IL 60606
www.worldability.org

Appendix C

RESOURCES: Character Education

Organizations

Center for the Advancement of Ethics and Character
Boston University School of Education
621 Commonwealth Avenue
Boston, MA 02215
(617) 353-3262
www.bu.edu/sed/caec

Center for the 4th and 5th R's
SUNY Cortland School of Education
P.O. Box 2000 • Cortland, NY 13045
(607) 753-2455
www.cortland.edu/character

The Center for Social and Emotional Education
1841 Broadway, Suite 713
New York NY 10023
(212) 707-8799
www.csee.net

CHARACTERplus
8225 Florissant Road
St. Louis, Missouri 63121
(800) 835-8282
www.characterplus.org

Character Counts! Coalition
4640 Admiralty Way #1001 Dpt. 50
Marina Del Ray, CA 90292-6610
(607) 753-2456
www.charactercounts.org

Character Education Partnership
1025 Connecticut Avenue NW, Suite 1011
Washington, DC 20036
(800) 988-8081
www.character.org

Collaborative for Academic, Social, Emotional Learning (CASEL)
Department of Psychology (M/C 285)
University of Illinois at Chicago
1007 W. Harrison St.
Chicago, IL 60607-7137
(312) 413-1008
www.casel.org

Community of Caring, Inc.,
1901 E. South Campus Drive #1120
Salt Lake City, Utah 84112
(801) 587-8990
www.communityofcaring.org

Educators for Social Responsibility
23 Garden Street
Cambridge, MA 02138
(617) 492-1764
www.esrnational.org

International Center for Character Education
University of San Diego
Division of Continuing Education
5998 Alcala Park
San Diego, CA 92110-2492
(619) 260-5980
www.teachvalues.org

Jefferson Center for Character Education
P.O. Box 4137
Mission Viejo, CA 92690-4137
(949) 770-7602
www.jeffersoncenter.org

Josephson Institute of Ethics
9841 Airport Blvd., #300
Los Angeles, CA 90045
(800) 711-2670
www.josephsoninstitute.org

Six Seconds
316 Seville Way
San Mateo, CA 94402
(650) 685-9885
www.6seconds.org

Appendix D

MRI of Callosal Agenesis: Midline Sagittal View

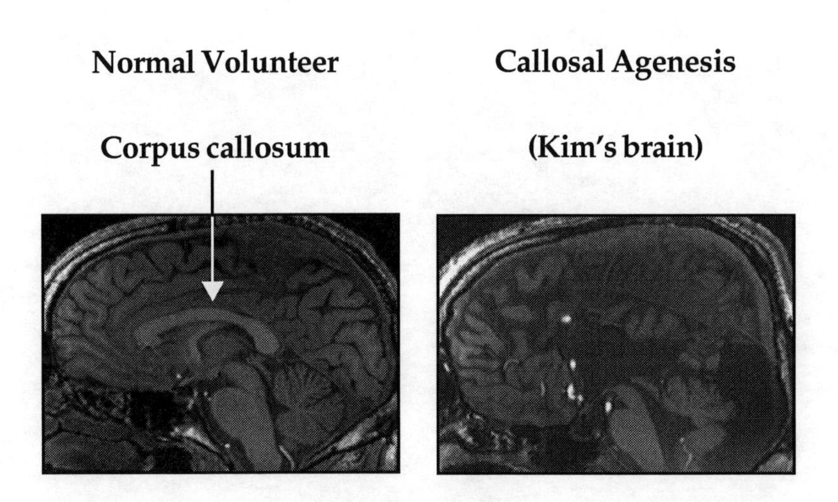

The above MRI scans were provided by Pratik Mukherjee, MD, PhD, University of California, San Francisco. They previously appeared in the December 2005 *Scientific American* article cited in the reference section. Left scan shows a normal brain; right scan shows Kim's brain, with the absence of a corpus callosum.